Praise for *Succeeding with Open Source*

"Open source software is transforming the way companies acquire and manage software at every level, from operating systems to applications. Today, IT managers who don't evaluate open source alternatives to proprietary software are doing their companies a profound disservice. If you are involved in any aspect of software acquisition and you aren't intimately familiar with how open source systems are created, documented, and supported, you need this book. It provides you with a new framework for assessing the maturity of open source solutions, walks you through every step of the evaluation process, and provides vital insights into the risks and benefits of making the open source decision."

> — David A. Taylor, Ph.D., author of *Object Technology: A Manager's Guide* and *Supply Chains: A Manager's Guide*

"Novell, its customers, and its partners have been waiting for something like this: a quantitative and qualitative way to assess the strength of open source projects we hope to support or build into our products. Golden provides a clear, concise methodology for determining whether an open source project is enterprise-ready and what it would take to make it so."

> — Chris Stone, Vice Chairman, Novell

"Open source software addresses many of the needs of IT organizations. While more and more organizations are using open source software, few understand how to evaluate it in the absence of a parent organization. Golden provides an effective mechanism to quickly evaluate open source software based on standard software measures—such as quality, support, and documentation—and to share those evaluations with other organizations. Using Golden's model, IT organizations can efficiently compare proprietary solutions to open source software solutions."

> — Stormy Peters, Open Source Program Office, Hewlett-Packard Company

"This book contains some of the most valuable, practical advice I have seen on how to transform the use of open source software from an accidental process into a powerful strategy for gaining an edge on the competition. By providing measurable engineering and process criteria for selecting open source products and processes, it brings open source software and methods squarely within the fold of traditional software engineering and business practices. I believe this book will be looked back on as an important transition point for recognizing how open source software can be used to promote business innovation and control costs."

— Terry Bollinger, IT Analyst, The MITRE Corporation, author of "Use of Free and Open Source Software in the U.S. Department of Defense," and former editor of *IEEE Software* magazine

"An outstanding look at how open source software can provide both a competitive edge and significant cost savings for any company. Required reading for any technical professional or manager."

— Kevin Bedell, Editor in Chief, *LinuxWorld Magazine*

"This book describes a thorough and pragmatic process to determine if/when an organization should employ open source software in mission-critical systems. Golden's Open Source Maturity Model is a vital tool for planning open source successes."

— Craig Murphy, Chief Technology Officer, Sabre

Succeeding with Open Source

Bernard Golden

✦Addison-Wesley

Boston • San Francisco • New York • Toronto
Montreal • London • Munich • Paris • Madrid
Capetown • Sydney • Tokyo • Singapore • Mexico City

The publisher offers discounts on this book when ordered in quantity for bulk purchases and special sales. For more information, please contact:

U.S. Corporate and Government Sales
(800) 382-3419
corpsales@pearsontechgroup.com

For sales outside of the U.S., please contact:

International Sales
(317) 581-3793
international@pearsontechgroup.com

Visit Addison-Wesley on the Web: www.awprofessional.com

Library of Congress Cataloging-in-Publication Data

Golden, Bernard, 1953-
  Succeeding with open source / Bernard Golden.
    p. cm.
  Includes bibliographical references and index.
  ISBN 0-321-26853-9 (pbk. : alk. paper)
 1. Shareware (Computer software) 2. Open source
software. I. Title.

  QA76.76.S46G65 2004
  005.36—dc22

                                    2004010528

ISBN 0-321-26853-9
Text printed on recycled paper
1 2 3 4 5 6 7 8 9 10—CRW—0807060504
First printing, July 2004

To Alison, my North Star.

Contents

PART I
Overview of Open Source

1.
The Source of Open Source

2.
Open Source Business Models

3.
Open Source Risks

PART II
Selecting, Assessing, and Evaluating Open Source Software

4.
The Open Source Maturity Model

5.
The Open Source Product

6.

Open Source Technical Support

7.

Open Source Documentation

8.

Open Source Training

9.

Open Source Integration
with Other Products

10.

Open Source Professional Services

11.

JBoss Open Source
Maturity Model Assessment

Contents

Preface

This book grew out of work my system integration firm, Navica, performed for our clients. We serve both large and small companies in a variety of industries, implementing and configuring software applications as well as developing custom systems. It's not exactly a secret that IT budgets have been tight over the past few years, so many of our clients asked us to explore ways to deliver projects at lower cost.

In our efforts to find ways to lower project costs, we came across something called open source software. Given my background in large IT shops, global consulting firms, and enterprise software companies, I was pretty skeptical about a product that promised something for nothing. The whole ethos of volunteers delivering high-quality software seemed counterintuitive to me. Furthermore, I wondered how we could obtain support and training for the product. In short, I couldn't understand how open source worked. However, I felt we had to try open source as part of our effort to do the best possible job for our clients.

Our experience with open source amazed us. Far from our nightmare vision of poor quality code distributed by a flaky group of unqualified idealists, we found that robust products were available that performed more than adequately—we were able to succeed with open source. I knew we were onto something when our clients began to ask, "What other open source software can we use in our system?"

This presented us with another problem. Many of our clients accepted without question our open source recommendations; after all, the role of a professional services firm is to serve as a trusted advisor, and these clients expected us to fulfill that role. Others, however, although not mistrusting us, would inquire how we chose the proposed product. If the project plan called for turning the system over to them after implementation, they would ask about training options and quality, where they could turn for support, and so on. Even though we had seen good results with the products we recommended, we really had no formal criteria or documentation we could point to as the basis for our recommendation. The problem was compounded if our clients needed to get approval for the project from higher-ups in the organization. The higher you go in an organization, the more formal the paperwork needs to be. It wasn't nearly enough to present a slide that, under selection criteria, stated "a guy from the system integrator heard this was a good open source product." Clearly, our clients needed something more concrete for their project approval and budget process.

Even if our clients would have accepted an informal method of selecting open source products for their projects, I was uncomfortable with it. A career spent creating and implementing mission-critical software has made me acutely aware of the importance of assessing software in all its dimensions: functionality, support, training, and documentation, among others. If we were going to recommend open source products as a key piece of our client's software infrastructure, I felt we needed a more formal methodology that would assess a product along all of those dimensions *before* we put it into production.

Out of that came our development of the Open Source Maturity Model (OSMM). This model assesses open source products for their maturity—essentially, their production-readiness. The OSMM enables one or two people to evaluate an open source product with less than a week's work. By doing so, the model quickly identifies which products are worth a more in-depth pilot-project evaluation. Using the model has made us more comfortable with our recommendations, made our clients' project-approval process flow much more easily, and significantly reduced our clients' project risk.

As we've created open source–based systems for our clients, I've concluded that all IT users share their motivations. Open source is going to be widely used throughout the industry. Its cost structure is compelling. I believe the move to open source is consistent with the cost-reduction trend in all industries via customer self-service and self-reliance. As an example, look at the airline industry. In the beginning, it delivered high-cost, full-service transportation, complete with elegant meals and personal attention. Today, airplanes get you there just as fast, but elegance is but a distant memory. Passengers book their own tickets on the Internet (Remember travel agents? Another victim of self service. . .), bring their own meals, and pay extra for a movie, all in the name of low fares. You'll occasionally hear someone nostalgically recalling the long-gone days of elegant airline travel, usually a passenger about to step onto a Southwest Airlines jet—the Greyhound bus of the sky. The obvious IT analogy is the hardware transformation driven by Dell. You get a rock-bottom price but are expected to install and configure the system yourself. I believe software is going to tread that same path: low prices (free in the case of open source) accompanied by more do-it-yourself work.

Because of this belief, I decided to share our experiences with open source. As it becomes more widely used, a formalized method of selecting and assessing open source software and all of its elements will be extremely useful. You can take advantage of the system we use and shorten your learning curve with open source products. There is no turning back: You will need to be more self-reliant in the future as you choose and implement software. I hope you find the material in this book useful. If you do (or, for that matter, if you don't), I would be delighted to hear from you; I can be reached at *bgolden@navicasoft.com*. More information about the OSMM and the book, including additional OSMM assessments of open source software as they are prepared, is available at *www.navicasoft.com*. Please visit the site to view the latest information.

Acknowledgments

To a writer, a book often seems like a child: a source of pride, frustration, hope, and despair—sometimes simultaneously. As a former First Lady observed, it takes a village to raise a child. The village offers help to the parent, wisdom to the child, and continuity to the family. A book also benefits from the participation of many people who offer perspective, experience, and encouragement to the writer. This book is certainly no exception to the challenges that all books go through, and it benefited enormously from help and input I received during its writing.

I would like to extend my deep gratitude to the following individuals:

Mary O'Brien, Robin O'Brien, John Fuller, and Brenda Mulligan of Addison-Wesley. Mary first believed in the proposal, and she and the others helped bring it to life.

Greg Kelleher, whose excellent perspective of open source developed as a Linux evangelist for IBM, helped me ensure that the concerns of mainstream IT organizations were addressed in the book.

Stan Gibson of *eWeek* and chromatic of O'Reilly Press who published the original articles from which this book's content was developed.

Patrick McGovern, director of SourceForge, who offered me lots of information about the site and its inner workings.

Dave Wasshausen of the Bureau of Economic Analysis, U.S. Department of Commerce, who helped me understand the magnitude, patterns, and trends in information technology capital investment.

Craig Hughes, Jeremy Allison, and John Terpstra, who described their projects in depth and offered many observations about open source from the perspective of developers.

Bob Bickel of JBoss, who unhesitatingly agreed to allow me to use the product as the OSMM example in the book, without any attempt to affect my assessment or scoring of the product. I truly appreciate his support and hands-off approach.

Maureen Dorney of GrayCary, Larry Rosen of the Open Source Initiative, Jason Wacha of MontaVista and Open-Bar.org, and Hank Jones III, attorneys all, who offered input and guidance about the ins and outs of open source licenses.

Kevin Dick, David Taylor, Kackie Cohen, and John Addison, writers who gave me inspiration, advice, and insight about the business of putting a book together. David was especially helpful in developing the original proposal and tightening up the organization of the manuscript, and for that I am very grateful.

Russell Brand, Sunia Yang, Casey Wimsatt, Roger Magoulas, Rupert Hart, and Mike Jarrett, friends and colleagues who reviewed the manuscript and gave many suggestions for improving the book.

And, most of all, Alison, Sebastian, and Oliver, who despite offering constant entertaining distractions, made writing the book a delight.

Introduction

Information technology (IT) organizations face a cruel world today. On one hand, there is relentless pressure to cut costs; on the other, an unending demand for innovative solutions. Like Odysseus' band of sailors who had to steer between the two perils of Scylla and Charybdis, IT organizations must steer a middle course. However, they face a situation much worse than the one that threatened the Greeks. Odysseus merely had to avoid either fate, but IT organizations must satisfy both! Put in more contemporary terms, like Miller Lite beer, which promises to be both less filling and taste great, to succeed today, IT must both cut costs and deliver innovation.

The pressure to cut costs stems from several factors. Over the past four years, U.S. capital spending has plummeted to a degree never before seen; IT spending has suffered as part of this trend. Beyond this specific economic effect, IT's role has been called into question as well. The denigration of IT's importance was most starkly portrayed in the May 2003 *Harvard Business Review* article by Nicholas G. Carr, "IT Doesn't Matter." In it, Carr drew historical parallels to railroads and electric power, noting that, while they conferred competitive advantage to their early users, they soon became undifferentiated infrastructure—something all entrants in a market used equally well. He has since followed the article up with a book titled *Does IT Matter?* IT organizations everywhere should be relieved that at least it is posed as a question, rather than a flat imperative. One hopes his prescriptions have moved beyond those in the original article, where he recommended longer durations between PC upgrades and rationing user disk space. These hardly seem the stuff of a *Harvard Business Review* cover article. Harvard Press might be hedging its bet on this topic; one month after releasing *Does IT Matter?* they released *IT Governance*, which proves that "Firms with superior IT governance have twice the profit of firms with poor governance." Overall, Carr's work represents the view that IT should be managed to minimize its cost structure.

The Charybdis to Carr's Scylla (or, if you will, the "tastes great" to Carr's "less filling") is the demand for IT innovation. The voices insisting on the importance of IT innovation are perhaps more familiar to the readers of this book—they belong to the leaders of many well-known technology vendors. It's easy to dismiss their message as nothing more than the bleatings of men and women whose jobs depend on the frequent upgrades of hardware and software, but for a discipline that is putatively becoming less important, there sure seems to be a lot on IT's plate. This year it's Web services; next year it's Wi-Fi; the year after that, RFID will be a strategic imperative. I'm confident that, in three years' time, there will be a new set of critical innovations that need to be addressed immediately. Notwithstanding the self-interested proclamations of the industry's leaders, how can we understand this unending demand for innovation?

Carr's analysis falls short because IT is fundamentally different from trains, electric power, or, for that matter, automobiles, petroleum, health care, or any other sector of the economy. Why? Thank Messrs. Moore, Metcalfe, and Gilder.[1] Each of them has propounded a law, which, taken together, accounts for the relentless opportunity and demand for innovation. Moore's Law is the best known: The power of a chip doubles every 18 months or so. Just as important is the inverse: The cost of a given amount of computing power falls by half in the same time frame. This goes on year after year—more than 30 at last count—with no prospect of the rate changing any time soon. Metcalfe noted that the value of a network

---

1. Please go to *www.netlingo.com* for a full description of Moore's Law, Metcalfe's Law, and Guilder's Law.

of connected devices increases at a geometrical rate even though the number of devices themselves only grows arithmetically. Gilder has been discredited because of the telecom bust, but he posited that available bandwidth for a fixed price would triple each year. This might not have been borne out, but certainly bandwidth is enormously less expensive today than it was in the recent past.

Because of these laws, technology functions that were prohibitively expensive a few short years ago are now financially viable. Wi-Fi, to take one example, would have been unaffordable five years ago; today you can buy an access point for $39 at your local electronics store. The ubiquity and cheapness of Wi-Fi makes the number of new devices (like Wi-Fi-enabled phones) much more valuable. Those phones will soon be connected by Voice over IP (VoIP), communicating across the Internet.

Carr's thesis is correct with respect to his historical examples. He merely failed to note the difference in type between his examples and IT. As an illustration, take railroads. He noted that within about 30 years of the invention of the railroad, its innovation was largely finished. Railroads became nothing more than a prosaic means to move people and goods. However, imagine if railroads had a Moore's law: Rather than the top speed of a railroad increasing from, say, 30 miles per hour to around 250 miles per hour today, the top speed of a railroad would have increased from 30 miles per hour in 1850 to 30,720 miles per hour in 1860! This would have changed railroads from a commodity transportation provider to something that would transform business operations, year after year after year. Consequently, I don't think IT's innovation and competitive advantage will disappear any time soon. If anything, it seems like whole new waves of innovation are becoming possible. One of the tricky things to keep in mind is that the increases get bigger the longer the doubling goes on.

There is one aspect of Carr's analysis of IT that is indisputably correct. He states flatly that IT is not going to increase its share of overall capital spending. IT accounted for about 10 percent of U.S. capital spending in 1970; today it represents about 38 percent, according to the Bureau of Economic Analysis. In other words, IT quadrupled its piece of the capital investment pie during the past third of a century. Its piece of the pie is not going to increase significantly in the future.

If demand for innovation continues (and perhaps continues to increase) and IT capital spending increases at no more than the rate of gross domestic product (GDP) growth, how can these two facts be reconciled? To my mind, the answer can only be this: IT will displace investment from commodity infrastructure to innovative applications through the use of open source software. Only by reducing spending in one area can the dollars be found to invest in another. Cost pressures will motivate IT organizations to pursue open source solutions; within two years I believe that every software selection process will ask the question, "Is there an open source option available?" The answer will not always be yes, and shouldn't always be yes, but the question will be asked. The use of software will change more over the next five years than it has in the past 40 years.

It will not be a painless transition. Open source is a relatively new phenomenon, widely misunderstood by technology vendors, technology users, and, perhaps surprisingly, by many open source developers themselves. In fact, here is my list of the top five open source myths:

Myth Number 1: Open source means Linux. The stars have aligned for Linux. Several of the largest technology vendors are pushing Linux relentlessly, more for market share advantage against their competitors than a burning desire to support open source. Users are benefiting tremendously from this push and are beginning to respond positively to the message of open source. Linux is rapidly becoming an accepted operating system choice for IT servers and even client machines. However, Linux is just one of more than 70,000 open source software products that are available. IT organizations will rapidly move to a world in which selecting open source products will be a commonplace task.

Myth Number 2: Open source only runs on Linux. Well, there might be a lot of open source products, but you must run Linux to take advantage of them, right? No. Most open source products run on a variety of operating systems. Even if you run another operating system, you can take advantage of open source.

Myth Number 3: Nobody runs open source in production. Many IT organizations believe, with fervent support from their commercial suppliers, that open source is not ready for demanding environments. There are certainly environments that are best suited to commercial products, but open source is definitely used in production systems. If you've used Amazon or Google, you've experienced production use of open source. Open source will increasingly be used in production environments.

Myth Number 4: Open source will destroy the software industry. Some vendors assert that open source is anticapitalist and should not be available because it will ruin the software industry. Some open source developers believe that open source solves all problems and will wipe out commercial vendors. Neither side is right. Open source developers are very good at developing infrastructure, but have not yet addressed industry-specific applications (verticals, as they're called). I'm not sure they ever will. In any case, the availability of free software will increase the use of software dramatically. I learned this during my MBA studies, where I saw countless demand curves increasing as the cost of goods dropped. Open source software in the infrastructure will increase demand higher up in the application stack. I refer to this as "innovation moves to the edge," edge being defined as new software-enabled technologies (like Wi-Fi) or business-oriented applications that will garner capital investment.

Myth Number 5: Open source is just like commercial software. This is tempting to believe—after all, software is software, right? Wrong! Open source software is created differently, distributed differently, and operated differently. The theme of this book is that open source users must prepare for a much more do-it-yourself world with respect to open source. The fact that it's free means that product elements formerly delivered by vendors will now need to be sourced by users.

Although I believe open source will have an enormous impact on the creators and users of software, I approach open source use very pragmatically. This book is designed to assist IT groups as they use open source. IT organizations can succeed with open source, but only if they recognize its differences from commercial software and the new practices it requires.

To that end, this book is organized into two parts.

Part 1, Chapters 1 through 3, provides an overview of open source, a review of open source business models, and a discussion of open source risks. If you are already familiar with open source, you might not need to read these chapters, but it might be worth your while. The topic of open source licensing is addressed in the risks chapter.

Part 2, Chapters 4 through 11, addresses how to select, assess, and evaluate open source software, because the control users now have is matched with increased responsibility. The Open Source Maturity Model (OSMM) is presented to enable organizations to quickly determine whether an open source product is mature enough for production use. These chapters form the heart of the book and address the topics of technical support, training, and documentation, as well as other product elements. Most organizations will use open source as is, even though code is available for modification, if desired. Therefore, determining how mature a product is, as it stands, will be critical for IT organizations. This part of the book will assist them in this determination.

If you've read the preface, you've seen that this book springs from my firm's experience with open source software. I've attempted to crystallize the lessons we've learned so that others can shorten their learning curves (and avoid many of the mistakes we made along the way). I hope you find it useful and enjoyable.

PART

I

Overview of Open Source

1

The Source
of Open Source

Executive Summary

Every good newspaper story starts with these critical questions: who, what, when, where, why, and how. By answering these questions right up front, the reporter enables readers to comprehend the important facts and implications of an issue quickly and incisively. This chapter uses the practices of journalism to provide a quick overview of open source software. It addresses each of the questions and offers a speedy introduction to what is perhaps the biggest sea change in the software industry since its beginnings more than 40 years ago.

This chapter answers the who, what, when, where, why, and how of open source.

Since those beginnings, nearly every software company in the world has followed the same business archetype: closely held intellectual property, developed by the company's own employees, delivered in binary format, licensed to users to run on their own computers. This formula has been responsible for the growth of today's commercial software industry: a $400-billion business behemoth that the United States dominates, and the products of which impact nearly every person on earth.

Software has traditionally followed a consistent business archetype.

Today, however, that archetype is being challenged by a new software formula: open source. Developed and maintained by volunteers, distributed to users at no cost, and available in source form, it is radically different from its commercial counterpart. Open source promises to shift the balance of power from vendors to users: Information technology (IT) organizations can, for the first time, control their own destiny.

Open source differs radically from commercial software and offers users much more control.

Open source's control comes with new responsibilities.

However, this control comes with a price. As the story of Aladdin and the magic lamp illustrates, magic powers carry with them new responsibilities. Each of the new characteristics of open source software forces IT organizations to develop new ways of thinking about how they procure and implement software.

Open source offers IT organizations much more freedom.

Available without cost, open source is distributed to users under different licensing terms from commercial software. Open source licenses offer IT organizations much more freedom in how they use software—freedom to install it wherever they want, modify its source code if they wish, and even redistribute the modified source to anyone they choose. IT organizations have far more power over their software infrastructure now than at any time in the history of computing.

Open source is created much differently from commercial software.

In addition to the different license conditions, open source software is created under different conditions from commercial software. Instead of being developed by a private company that takes responsibility for all aspects of the product, open source is written by a small group of developers, typically unpaid volunteers. For delivery of all other product elements, open source developers rely on the user community or other commercial entities.

Open source causes IT organizations to use new methods to select and assess software.

Because of the differences between open source and commercial software, IT organizations must use new methods to select and assess software. Open source users must take responsibility for locating all the product elements that commercial software companies typically deliver along with their software: support, training, documentation, and the like.

With open source, users must take responsibility for the quality of the complete product.

Locating the elements is just half the battle, however. Unlike the commercial software industry, where the vendor takes responsibility for the quality of each of the product elements, in the open source world that responsibility falls to the user. Each element must be evaluated by the user to determine its quality. This responsibility demands a new model of product procurement—one where the IT organization is an active participant in creating the complete product, rather than a passive recipient of what the vendor delivers.

The new archetype demands new working practices. Just as the software industry has had more than 40 years to perfect its business practices, software users have had more than 40 years to hone their skills in procuring and implementing commercial software. For open source, new skills need to be developed and used.

> The new open source archetype demands new working practices.

This chapter begins the process of outlining those skills with an introduction to open source. It addresses the following topics:

- What is open source?
- Who creates open source?
- Who uses open source?
- Where do I get open source software?
- When and how do I use open source?

What Is Open Source?

When most people hear the term *open source,* their initial reaction is, "What is open source? What does it mean?" Simply put, open source is software that has the following characteristics:

Source Code Availability

Open source is software that has source code available to its users. It can be downloaded at will and used or modified as desired, as long as its license requirements are observed. This differs significantly from commercial, or proprietary, software, which is distributed only in binary format to ensure that its intellectual property

> Open source means that the product's source code is available to all users.

remains privately held by the software creators. Commercial software is delivered in frozen form: It must be used as delivered.

Open source products are usually available in binary form as well.

Open source products are usually also available in binary form so that they can be used on common operating systems without needing to be compiled first. Of course, not every operating system will have a binary available, but the source code makes it possible for the product to be compiled for any operating system that does not have a binary version available.

Open source licenses impose far fewer restrictions on users.

Open source software licenses are far less restrictive in terms of how the software can be used. This does not mean that there are no conditions imposed by open source licenses. Open source usually allows an organization to use the software in any way it desires, but often requires that any changes made in the source code be shared with the user community and given to any customers of the organization that makes the change.

Zero-Price Software

Open source is usually available without charge.

Open source software is distributed at no cost (this is mostly true; see Chapter 2, "Open Source Business Models," for a discussion of open source products available for purchase). This makes sense because it reflects the reality of source code availability. There is no way to control distribution of a software product available in source form. If any attempt were made to limit the product's use by, for example, locking the executable onto a single processor, the source could be modified to take out that portion of the code. Free source implies zero-price software.

Open source is different from freeware.

There is no charge for the source code either. In this way, open source differs significantly from *freeware,* a type of software open source is often confused with. Freeware is software distributed without a fee, but without source code access. Freeware creators tightly restrict the intellectual property rights to the software and offer the software on a "take it as it is" basis, in contrast to open source, which carries far less restrictive licensing terms and allows users to modify the product if they so desire.

Freeware is often distributed on a "time-bombed" basis, meaning it is free for use for a certain period of time. When that period is up, the software stops working. If the user wants to continue using the product, a licensing fee is necessary to defuse the "time-bomb" restriction.

The fact that open source software is zero price offers tremendous benefits to users:

- The common dilemma of wanting more installations than they can afford is avoided. Use of additional copies often increases the benefits of the software to the organization.
- The availability of zero-price software encourages innovation. Expensive software forces IT organizations to purchase software only for proven applications. Lower costs allow organizations to experiment and develop new applications or even new lines of business. This allows an organization to take greater advantage of IT in running their business.
- Zero-price software enables IT organizations to stretch their budgets farther and purchase software that they might not have been otherwise able to afford. The dollars saved by using free software allows funding for additional applications that might not have otherwise made the budgetary cut.
- Zero-price software reduces overall IT costs, allowing an organization to make greater investments in other aspects of its business. Free software reduces the number of capital expenditure trade-offs that companies must make.

FREE SOFTWARE AND ZERO-PRICE SOFTWARE

Readers who wonder why the unusual "zero price" term is used instead of "free" should be aware that some participants in the open source community have a very different meaning for the term "Free Software." The adherents of Free Software believe that computer software should be widely available with no restrictions placed on its use, study, copy, modification, or redistribution.

Most participants in the open source community do not share these beliefs, but instead feel that intellectual property should be made available according to the motivation of the creator(s). Much more information about Free Software can be found at the Free Software Foundation's Web site (*www.fsf.org*).

It might seem a bit confusing to use the term zero price to refer to the cost of open source software, but this alternative seems preferable to the potential confusion of using the term free. The term Free Software carries with it much more implication than zero price, which should be kept in mind. In this text, zero price refers explicitly to the fact that most open source products are available at no charge.

Open Source: A Different Licensing Model

Software licenses protect the intellectual property of the creator(s).

All software licenses reflect the rights of the creator to control how the software is distributed. Software is a copyrighted entity that embodies intellectual property, and, as such, enjoys the legal protection of copyright law. Although copyright law is often used to restrict use of a product, the law can be used to enable wide distribution as well. Every piece of software is distributed under some kind of license, which controls the manner in which the product can be used.

Open source licenses are significantly different from commercial software licenses.

Open source licenses differ significantly from commercial software licenses. Commercial licenses restrict the use of the software as much as possible, to enhance the possibility of selling many licenses. In contrast, open source licenses are written with the aim of encouraging wide use, with very few restrictions placed on the use of the software.

One way of viewing the differences in licensing practices between commercial and open source is that commercial software licenses are written to allow the software creators to harvest the value that users receive from the product. By contrast, open source licenses are written to allow software users to harvest the value from the product. As noted earlier, users are allowed to modify the source code if they desire to increase the value they receive from the software. Other benefits of open source licensing include the following:

- Users are not restricted as to which or on how many machines they can install software. Commercial licenses typically control very tightly on how many machines software can be used. Being able to install as many copies as desired is a great benefit to users. As application use grows, it is easy to expand the number of copies installed for load-balancing purposes. Furthermore, organizations can install additional copies of open source software for training, testing, demonstration, and integration purposes. The flexible licensing terms encourage organizations to use software in ways that offer the greatest benefit to them. Strict licensing terms often restrict users from using software in ways that offer them the greatest possible benefit.
- There are no restrictions on access to later versions of the software. Commercial software licenses often require large "maintenance" payments to enable user organizations to access patches, maintenance releases, and upgrade versions of the software. Open source software imposes no such restrictions.
- The user communities for open source products are usually much larger than for commercial products. Because the products are available at zero price, many more organizations use the products. Large user communities offer many benefits to the developers and users of the software.

Open Source: Free Speech, Not Free Beer

"Free speech, not free beer" embodies the beliefs of open source.

Open source devotees often describe the importance of its licensing with the phrase "free speech, not free beer." The point of this phrase is that, although open source software is usually available at zero price, the critical aspect about it is that open source offers real freedom for software creators and users. Specifically, the "free speech" part of the epigram refers to the liberty that the users of open source have to use, modify, and distribute the software. This liberty is tied to the licensing conditions that make source code available to software users.

"Free speech, not free beer" emphasizes the rights that accompany open source.

Source availability means that the uses someone can make of software are nearly unlimited. It can be copied. It can be modified for one's own purposes. The modified version can be distributed as well, if one chooses to do so. So, "free speech, not free beer" emphasizes the rights that accompany open source licenses and points out that these rights are not the same thing as zero-price software.

Not all users are focused on the free speech part of "free speech, not free beer."

"Free speech, not free beer" might overstate the appeal of free speech and understate the appeal of zero-price software to most open source users, just as New Hampshire's motto "Live Free or Die" might be only a small part of the residents' enjoyment of the state—the larger part being the low taxes they pay. However, open source licensing terms make possible the free availability of products as well as underlying the other benefits of open source software. The topic of Free Software is addressed in the "Free Software and Zero-Price Software" sidebar as well as in the licensing section of Chapter 3, "Open Source Risks."

Conditions of Open Source Licensing

Open source does carry licensing restrictions.

Just because open source products are available with an unrestrictive license does not mean that there are no licensing conditions at all. Typical license conditions include contributing any source changes back to the main source base and distributing source changes to any customers of the organization that modified the code. The specific conditions depend on the type of open source license that accompanies a given product. The topic of open source licensing is addressed at greater length in Chapter 3, "Open Source Risks."

Who Creates Open Source?

A consistent question regarding open source is, "Who writes open source software?" A second, often-unasked question is, "Why would anyone work on open source?" Many people don't understand why someone would program without financial compensation, because they view programming as unfulfilling drudgery. Alternatively, many people believe that open source developers must be students or unemployed, with an assumption that they work on open source in place of a real job.

A key question is, "Who creates open source and why do they do it?"

Who creates open source software and how they support their work on open source is, however, key for pragmatic users. IT organizations need to use software that will be available and supported for the long term—their software infrastructure must be "future-proof." Relying on software created by people who are uncommitted for the long term is too risky. After all, no IT organization wants to find that a key piece of technology is suddenly orphaned because the developers lost interest or had to "get a real job."

IT organizations view the ongoing involvement of developers as key to software success.

Of course, the availability of source code makes a product future-proof in some sense. Even if the developers end their involvement with an open source product, users have the source code itself to rely on for use in the future. This really isn't enough for most IT organizations, however. Almost all commercial enterprise software purchases come with source code escrow agreements, which make the product source available if the vendor goes out of business. IT organizations avoid doing business with vendors when they suspect

Source code access is not usually enough for pragmatic IT organizations.

the escrow conditions might come into play, however. IT organizations want working software, not a code base. Source code escrow arrangements are a last resort, not a procurement strategy.

Even with source availability, the question of who creates open source remains.

Therefore, most IT organizations do not perceive the source availability of open source products as their path forward. Even those that work with source code want to contribute to ongoing product development rather than taking on sole responsibility for the product. Therefore, the question of who creates open source software remains key. Who are open source developers? Can they be relied on to create a long-lived product?

A good profile of open source developers and development practices is available.

Fortunately, there is good information available about the open source development community. In 2002, the Boston Consulting Group (BCG)[1] carried out a large survey of the open source community in cooperation with SourceForge, an open source portal. They did this to better understand the potential of open source as well as how much risk is present for open source users. BCG contacted more than 1,500 randomly chosen open source developers with a Web-based survey and received more than 500 responses. The findings of the survey provided a snapshot of the open source development community; more important, the findings contradicted the assumptions many people have about open source developers. (The complete findings of the survey can be found at *www.osdn.com/bcg/*.)

---

1.   "The Boston Consulting Group Hacker Survey," presented at the O'Reilly Open Source Conference, San Diego, CA, July 24, 2002. Available at *www.bcg.com/opensource/BCGHackerSurveyOSCON24July02v073.pdf*.

Why Do Developers Work on Open Source?

BCG found that open source developers are motivated by intellectual curiosity and a desire to improve their skills. Many of them consider programming to have an aesthetic appeal, like poetry or music. For these developers, working on open source is far from a burden; it is a chance to do something they find personally fulfilling. In fact, a majority of them agreed that "when I program, I lose track of time" and that "with one more hour in the day, I would spend it programming." A large proportion of the respondents also felt a sense of personal accomplishment by working on open source.

Open source developers consider programming a mode of self-expression.

With respect to the issue of risk being posed by the developers of a project abandoning it, a significant percentage believe that one of the requirements of working on open source is finding someone to take on the project if a developer leaves it. Developers begin contributing to an open source product out of a sense of interest and typically develop a personal stake in their work. For that reason, they are unlikely to abandon a product without seeing that someone else is ready to take over their role. Still, there is some risk that one or more members of the development team might walk away from a product, leaving users exposed.

Open source developers consider continuity of their project very important.

What Are Open Source Developers Like?

To a large degree, open source developers reflect a trend that has been noted in many other professions: stronger identification with peer professionals than with organizations. An overwhelming majority—83 percent—agreed strongly or agreed somewhat with the statement, "Hackers are a primary community with which I identify." It should be noted that, in this context, *hackers* refers to very technically oriented individuals and not to people with malicious motivations.

Open source developers identify most strongly with their profession.

The survey respondents were mostly between 20 and 30 years of age and 98 percent were male. They averaged 11 years of professional IT experience.

In terms of geographic location, North America is home to approximately 46 percent of open source developers, Europe accounts for about 42 percent of developers, and the remaining 12 percent are located in other areas of the world.

The geographic distribution of open source developers is different from open source users.

Interestingly, this distribution of developers does not match the distribution of open source users. About 24 percent of all downloads from SourceForge are from Internet domains located in the United States, with the remainder going to international domains. In terms of individual countries, page views (a proxy for downloads) identify the three heaviest user nations of SourceForge other than the United States as Germany, Canada, and the United Kingdom.

How Do Open Source Developers Support Themselves?

This is the question implied in the second question listed at the start of this section: "Why would anyone work on something for free?" Two surprising results came out of the BCG survey:

- A full 30 percent of those surveyed participate in open source development as part of their employment. These developers work in organizations that use open source products and they participate in the project to make the product work better for their employer's needs.
- Well over 50 percent of those surveyed are professionally employed in technology organizations. About 20 percent of those surveyed are students, with 7 percent being academics, and 15 percent identified as "other."

Therefore, most participants in open source development already work on technology. Their involvement in an open source project usually is in addition to their "real" job, motivated by skill development or the opportunity to work on an intellectually stimulating project. By no means are the participants only students or the unemployed.

Although the majority of open source developers already have full-time technology jobs, they devote a significant amount of time to their open source efforts. Volunteer participants (those who do not work on open source as part of their regular employment) contribute almost 6 hours per week to open source work, whereas those who are paid participants contribute a little more than 11 hours per week.

Open source developers devote significant time to their open source activities.

Implications of the BCG Survey

The BCG survey provides an excellent overview of the open source development world. Most open source developers are IT professionals who work on projects to improve their skills or for intellectual stimulation. Far from the stereotype of inexperienced or unemployable engineers, open source project developers have significant IT experience. They are usually employed in technology jobs and are unlikely to abandon a product and leave its users in the lurch. Open source developers have a strong commitment to the product and are reluctant to see its users harmed in any way. Consequently, the risk associated with using a product created by volunteers is probably not as high as many potential open source users believe.

Far from the stereotype of unemployed engineers, most open source developers have significant IT experience and are employed full-time in technology positions.

Who Uses Open Source?

The short answer is "everyone." If you've searched with Google, purchased books from Amazon, or placed a call with MCI, you've used open source. Each of these organizations uses open source as part of its core computing infrastructure.

Open source is used by a number of major corporations.

Many other corporations are actively experimenting with open source.

The somewhat longer answer is that many organizations currently use, are actively experimenting with, or are thinking about using open source. To date, users of open source have mostly been early adopters; pragmatic IT organizations are now beginning to consider open source, mostly for the reasons outlined earlier. A detailed discussion of how these early adopters and pragmatic organizations use IT is contained in Chapter 4, "The Open Source Maturity Model."

An open source product's user group is usually called its *community*.

The even longer answer is that open source is used by the product's user community. This might seem redundant, but the term *community* (or *user community*) is one you will hear repeatedly in discussions about open source. One of the key differences between commercial software and open source is captured in this phrase. To understand it, you need to consider the relationship between developer and user.

Commercial software developers are not usually accessible to the product community.

With commercial software, there is practically no interaction between software developers and the people who actually use the product. Most companies seek to shield their developers from users to enable them to focus full time on banging out the code needed for the next release.

Open source developers are usually highly involved with the product community.

In contrast, on open source projects, there is a great deal of interaction between developers and product users. In fact, one might say that there is a very intense relationship among all individuals involved with the product—whether developers or users. E-mails fly back and forth among the development team and product users. Feedback is sought and freely given. Without romanticizing community, it's critical to understand it and recognize how you can interact with it and take advantage of it. It's worth a discussion about community to see how it impacts how you will use open source. The place to begin community lies with the development team and how they work. After that, we can explore how the user community affects and is affected by open source.

OPEN SOURCE: TWO CASE STUDIES

Many people believe that open source software is not used in mission-critical production applications. Here are two examples of companies that rely on open source to run their mission-critical applications.

Charles Schwab

Charles Schwab runs a very large Web site that allows customers to buy and sell financial instruments, check the status of their accounts, and research potential investment opportunities. Traffic to the site varies enormously, depending on what is happening in the stock market on any given day. In the past, maintaining sufficient reserve computing capacity was difficult because of the high cost of the hardware. Over the past year, Schwab has been trading out proprietary UNIX boxes for inexpensive Intel-based machines running Linux. Geoff Penney, Schwab's chief information officer (CIO), states that the company had saved hundreds of thousands of dollars bringing in less-expensive machines. Moreover, it had also increased its ability to respond to traffic spikes, because it was now able to afford to have reserve capacity available.

Sabre

Sabre Holdings is a global travel company that operates the largest airline reservation system in the world. This system is so complex that its original mainframe systems ran an operating system written specifically for their application—the standard operating system couldn't handle the transaction load. Today Sabre not only operates this reservation system, but also offers software and services to travel organizations and airlines throughout the world. To reduce its operations costs, the company extensively uses open source software. Today, its core applications still reside on legacy systems, but they are surrounded by Linux-based servers using the open source database MySQL for storage, and communicate via the open source TAO object request broker. The services themselves are offered as Simple Object Access Protocol (SOAP)-based Web services that are constructed with open source software.

These applications perform hundreds of thousands of transactions each day, all of which execute on open source software systems. Sabre estimates that it has saved millions of dollars using open source software to enable external access to its core applications; in fact, because the airline industry has such thin margins, these applications would not have been economically feasible if the company used commercial software.

Created by Volunteers, Not Employees

Open source software is usually developed by volunteers.

Open source developers are typically IT professionals who donate their work on a voluntary basis (this is not universally true, as will be discussed in Chapter 2, "Open Source Business Models." By and large, however, most participants in an open source product are there by choice on an unpaid basis. In contrast, commercial software is written by paid employees.

The voluntary involvement of developers affects open source management practices.

The fact that open source is written by volunteers affects how open source product teams form and work. Because individuals participate based on their interest in the product, open source management practices are very different from those in commercial software companies.

Open source management practices require very different techniques.

Anyone who has worked in a voluntary organization will recognize the key differences between the two types of organizations. People volunteer for personal reasons, so getting individuals to work on something that doesn't interest them is fruitless. They won't do it—they just drift away. Volunteers must be emotionally engaged to work on a task and "managing" a volunteer is chiefly an exercise in figuring out a good way to motivate him or her. The role of a manager in an open source project involves lots of emotional stroking and personal interaction, which takes time and forfeits urgency. It can all seem very touchy-feely: There is no such thing as a well-disciplined voluntary organization.

Paid employees might not be as committed as one might think.

On the other hand, one might argue that the motivation of paid employees is less than complete. Just because an employer offers a paycheck doesn't mean that an employee is strongly motivated. Employees can accept their pay but disdain their tasks. Anyone who has spent time as a manager knows that some employees find it impossible to be enthusiastic about their work. If they're not enthusiastic, they deliver minimal effort. They might actually deliberately hinder their team's progress if they're unhappy enough. Therefore, it's important not to overstate the power that an employer has because it supports its employees' living standards.

There are tremendous benefits to having volunteers write open source software, however. Volunteers bring real passion to what they do. Again, anyone who has worked in a voluntary organization has seen the tremendous effort expended by participants. The inefficiencies in managing open source projects are balanced by the enthusiasm the engineers bring to the tasks they select. Great products are achieved by passion; it might not be missing in software written for pay, but it surely cannot be missing in software written for free.

> Volunteers' passionate commitment can lead to great products.

Because they are voluntary groups, open source development teams work together in a decentralized fashion with little hierarchy. The project leader is usually the individual who originated the project; he or she must manage by consensus with a "lead by example" approach. The project leader is responsible for developing a common understanding of what functionality the upcoming product release will contain, encouraging new developers to join the project, helping developers select a portion of the project to work on, and arbitrating any conflicts that arise between team members.

> Open source development teams work in a highly decentralized, consensus fashion.

In summary, egalitarian groups working together as volunteers create open source products. These groups operate with all the glories and frustrations that accompany any voluntary organization.

Development Practices

Open source projects tend to make early releases available for use by the user community and quickly refresh the releases as the product is modified. It's not unusual for new versions of a product under development to be released every few days. This practice is

> Open source projects "release early and often."

described as "release early and often." The open source community believes that this practice leads to higher-quality products.

"Release early and often" results in higher product quality.

The reasons for this belief are straightforward. Developers create and test code based on their assumptions about how it will be used. However, actual users use (and misuse) the product in ways that no developer could possibly have imagined. This use or misuse exercises unexpected code paths and stresses the code in unforeseen ways. By making the product widely available, a large pool of users quickly performs this product exercising and more quickly improves the product's quality.

Source code availability means that bug fixes are higher quality.

Because the source code for the product is available, a second factor comes into play. As the epigram "two heads are better than one" illustrates, additional perspectives about problems lead to better solutions. As many of the people using (or misusing) the product access the source code to create fixes that they then submit to the core development team, the overall solution created as a blend of the different fixes will be of higher quality than any one fix possibly could be. Certainly the use of a large pool of developers beyond the central team enables a broader perspective to be brought to bear on the source code. The benefit of having many people working on the source code is summarized in the open source shibboleth "many eyes make all bugs shallow." A side benefit of having many people looking at the source is that the code is reviewed for adherence to coding standards; fragile or inflexible code can also be improved as a result of these reviews. Generally speaking, code reviews are considered to be a very positive quality practice in software engineering.

Direct user feedback ensures that the product implements critical functionality.

A third factor that affects open source development practices is that large numbers of real users work with the product and offer feedback directly to the development team. This feedback enables the team to learn what features the product really needs to include to be more useful. By contrast, commercial product companies often suffer from what is known as *feature creep*, focusing on delivering more features in a race to outshine competitors rather than on what product users really need. There is no pithy catchphrase to express this open source practice, but the direct involvement of end users is believed to lead to more useful products.

A Philosophy of Community

The practice of frequent releases to gather user feedback highlights one of the most important aspects of the open source world: the community. The size and activity level of the community carries significant implications for organizations considering a product. Community pervades discussions of open source, and is discussed throughout this book. More particularly, the size and activity level of the community directly affects the maturity of the product. This book extensively addresses all the ways that the user community impacts the maturity of an open source product, and how you or your organization can use the user community to assess the product's maturity.

> One of the most important aspects of open source is the community.

What is an open source community? It is all the product developers, any users who are interested in participating, and any other individuals who care to be involved with a product. Essentially, it is a freewheeling organization of everyone who is interested in a particular product for whatever reason. There are no formal requirements for joining and no formal rules for participation.

> A product community is open to any interested participant.

However, lack of formality does not mean that there are no standards for participation or behavior. Very strong unwritten rules govern all community interactions. A community member is expected to interact respectfully, make reasoned arguments about why a particular course of action is right, and, above all, to contribute to as well as take advantage of the community.

> Easy participation does not imply lack of behavioral standards.

Open source product communities are very powerful and offer tremendous benefits:

- As described earlier, the interaction between developers and users makes for a more useful product. The product is better for having more people determining its direction and improving its stability via usage.
- The community offers a real resource to draw on for expertise in the product. It is very common for members of the community to help one another figure out problems or to suggest potential solutions for product usage.

There are some drawbacks, however:

- Because of the need for consensus and the large community size, the pace of work and decision making can seem very slow. There really isn't any way around this, but it usually doesn't cause an enormous problem. In any case, if you feel strongly about something, there is always source access to more quickly make changes that you feel are time sensitive.
- Despite the strong informal rules of participation, immature behavior sometimes (rarely, really) occurs. This can take the form of namecalling, but the more common form is one-upmanship based on technical opinion—the "it is obvious to anyone who really understands how objects interact that it should . . ." sort of thing.
- Occasionally, the community will engage in protracted discussions about off-topic subjects. Depending on your temperament, these discussions might be charming, mildly distracting, or irritatingly time wasting. I tend to the latter point of view, but have learned to grit my teeth because of the community benefits.

One unique aspect of an open source community is that it is essentially anonymous and extremely decentralized. Nearly all interaction is done via e-mail and Web forums. It is common for members of the development team to have never met, but to have worked together quite closely to create a high-quality product. Many members of a product community will cooperate to solve a problem successfully, all while being scattered literally around the world.

The community is anonymous and extremely decentralized.

Can Community Work?

Many IT managers are initially reluctant to use a product that relies so heavily on an informal community organization. They feel open source communities that lack hierarchical leadership and a formal governance structure must be inefficient and chaotic. It's easy to understand this reaction, because so much of corporate and governmental life revolves around hierarchies and formal rules of behavior.

Many IT managers question whether a community-based product can be successful.

At bottom, this reaction is based on a fear that community means no one is truly responsible for the product—that there is no one to turn to about a specific problem or an urgent need. There is a comforting sense that a commercial provider offers a responsible point of contact, sometimes charmingly referred to as "one throat to choke." On the other hand, having a commercial provider standing behind a product is no guarantee of responsible behavior. The software industry has witnessed many instances of companies abruptly declaring products "no longer supported" or defining them as having reached their "end of life plan." Another perspective on "one throat to choke" is "single point of failure," which is usually considered a bad thing.

Commercial practices are no guarantee of success, however.

However, there is a precedent for a technology successfully delivered by an informally structured organization. It is one that every reader of this book likely uses each day: the Internet. Despite its

The Internet itself is an example of a community-based success.

lack of formal hierarchy, use of the informal request for comment (RFC) standards mechanism, and reliance on personal reputation for leadership, the Internet has succeeded brilliantly. It is unlikely that a single commercial entity could have created what this informal organization has brought about. Many observers even argue that the lack of formal structure and regulations for the Internet have enabled it to evolve more quickly and be more useful than would otherwise have been possible.

Community is one of the benefits of open source software.

Many discussions about open source denigrate the commercial software world and describe open source methods as far superior and perhaps even better morally. The informal community is portrayed as delivering much better products that will eventually send commercial software to its deserved burial in the elephant's graveyard. My own view is that there are many powerful benefits available from using open source and the community is one of those benefits. I don't believe that commercial software is going to disappear by any means; however, I do believe that open source software will become an important part of every IT organization's infrastructure and that taking advantage of the community is vital to success with open source. Open source succeeds brilliantly at delivering software, and the community is an important part of that success.

Where Do I Get Open Source Software?

The most convenient place to get a product is from one of the open source portals.

Open source software is available from many different places. Individual open source products might have their own Web site to make the product available. There are several open source portals, which act as repositories of open source software. Many open source products are available at these portals, making them convenient for locating products via the portal's search capability. Finally, a few open source products are available for sale, typically made available by companies that have bundled the basic open source product along with some useful utilities and possibly an improved installation mechanism. Much more is said about commercial distributions in Chapter 2, "Open Source Business Models."

Individual Open Source Product Web Sites

Some very well established open source products have their own Web sites that act as the main distribution mechanism for the software. The Web sites act as gathering points for developers and the user community to interact. They often have forums for discussions and questions among the community. News about the product will be available as well. These Web sites are the electronic equivalent of an old-fashioned country store in which transactions, friendships, information swapping, and gossip all take place. The sites themselves can easily be found via a Google search on the product name.

Some open source products have their own Web site for distribution.

Open Source Portals

Open source portals offer a centralized location for open source products. The portals host open source projects, offering a number of services that make starting and maintaining an open source project much easier. As noted earlier, the fact that many projects are homed in a single portal offers real value to users, as they can easily search and sift through hundreds or even thousands of projects to find the right one. A fuller description of the services offered by the leading open source portal, SourceForge (*www.sourceforge.net*), is contained later in Chapter 5, "The Open Source Product."

SourceForge is an excellent open source portal.

SOURCEFORGE: AN OVERVIEW

SourceForge is a tremendous resource for open source users and developers. It offers a full range of services to developers, freeing them from creating project infrastructure. Instead, they can take advantage of what SourceForge provides.

One interesting question is how did SourceForge itself come into existence? Who took it upon themselves to create this community resource?

SourceForge was originally created by employees of VA Linux (now known as VA Software). VA Linux was a hotbed of open source activity centered on Linux, and SourceForge was a fairly informal portal set up as a casual project. However, as the number of projects grew, VA Linux recognized that the site needed to be robustly engineered to handle the traffic it was receiving. They put a team in charge that extended the functionality, implemented a scalable architecture, and planned future enhancements. SourceForge is now one of a number of open-source-oriented portals operated by OSDN, a subsidiary of VA Software.

Commercial Distributions

Some open source products are available on commercial distributions.

A few open source products are available for sale. I know that this sounds like a contradiction of the term open source, but commercial open source products do exist. The commercial product is usually offered along with other product-oriented services, like technical support or training. Even in the companies that offer a commercial version of an open source product, however, usually the product is available at zero price as well. The version sold is merely made available in a more convenient format (e.g., on a CD) or as part of a larger product offering that bundles services along with the software.

The Challenge of Anonymous Distribution

Open source products are available for anonymous download.

One of the most interesting, yet frustrating, aspects of open source is that not only is it available at zero price, but it is available anonymously. You don't have to identify yourself to download the product: no forms to fill in, no credit card information (unless the product is purchased), no nothing.

Anonymous download makes open source acquisition extremely easy.

This is absolutely a delight. Nothing stands between you and the product. You don't have to provide personal information to get the product. There is no need to go through an extended capital request cycle because the product costs nothing. Indeed, the easy availability can pose a problem, which is discussed in Chapter 3, "Open Source Risks."

On the other hand, it can be quite frustrating that the user base for an open source product is essentially faceless and nameless. Many times, the open source developers will have no idea of the identity of most of their users. Companies might be using the product as a key part of their software infrastructure, and no one will know. If you are assessing an open source product, this can pose quite a challenge. With a commercial product, you can ask to see customer references and talk with actual users to hear how the product has worked for them. In the open source world, it can be quite difficult to locate specific users to get the same information. There are ways to address this problem, which are discussed in Chapter 5, "The Open Source Product," but nonetheless the anonymity of open source can seem quite odd.

> Anonymous download means that many of a product's users will remain unknown.

When and How Do I Use Open Source?

These are intertwined questions. The right time to use open source is when both you and the product are ready. How to use open source is the subject of this book. The practices you (and the IT industry) have used over the past 40 years won't work with open source products. A whole new method of selecting and evaluating products is required to succeed with open source. The thesis of this book is that successful organizations will recognize that new methods are required and will implement them when they begin to work with open source.

> Using open source requires new working practices.

The next two chapters of the book address open source business models and open source risks. Chapter 4 starts off the discussion about how to succeed with open source. It outlines the types of technology users and why the key question users must ask about any open source product is, "How mature is it?"

> The key question for open source software is, "How mature is it?"

2

Open Source
Business Models

Executive Summary

Isn't the phrase "open source business model" an oxymoron? How can there be a business model for something that's given away for free? It might seem counterintuitive, but there are open source software companies that make a living selling open source products. Just as bottled water companies successfully market a product available at no cost or negligible cost from a convenient location (your kitchen tap), inventive entrepreneurs have created a number of business models based on open source software.

Although the vast majority of open source products are available only as free downloadable software, a number of open source products have commercial entities associated with them. To understand how you can take advantage of open source, it's important to understand the relationship between open source products and these entities.

The business strategy of these open source companies varies, and new strategies are being explored each day. If you are considering using open source in your software infrastructure, understanding the role of open source businesses is critical. The later chapters in the book extensively explore the impact commercial offerings have on the maturity of an open source product, so getting a grounding in open source business models is a key step in being ready to assess open source software.

Early Open Source Business Models:
By Enthusiasts for Enthusiasts

Open source is a relatively new development.

Open source hasn't been around that long. As a significant presence in the software world, open source has really only been available for a little over five years. However, even before open source became a recognized part of the software industry, there were passionate users of open source, especially Linux.

The first open source businesses were CD distributions of Linux.

Without making it sound like prehistory, early users typically used these products in severely limited hardware and connectivity environments. Home environments often had nothing more than dial-up access to the Internet, which significantly slowed download times. These conditions created the opportunity for the first open source businesses: CD distributions of Linux.

These businesses started small, but were a beginning for open source businesses.

Having CDs of Linux available for purchase allowed users to avoid the narrowband bottleneck affecting their download times. It also enabled Linux enthusiasts to support themselves through the sale of these CDs. These businesses were pretty small—usually no more than a few individuals—but they were a start.

These businesses were founded by enthusiasts for enthusiasts.

Linux at this time was the province of enthusiasts—individuals interested in bypassing commercial operating systems, willing to experiment with new software, and eager to share their experiences. The enthusiasts formed these businesses to make it easier for new users to get started; they were an outgrowth of their own passion for Linux. As people began to use the CD-based products, they would send questions about them back to the company; a free interchange of advice and knowledge went on constantly.

These businesses weren't terribly impressive, but they did (and do) help new users get their sea legs, in a way that allowed their founders to make a living.

The Next Model: Installation, Technical Support, and Consulting

It wasn't long before brave IT organizations began to play with open source products, paving the way for the next stage of open source businesses. The engineers who wrote early open source products assumed a highly technical user base—in other words, people like themselves. Unfortunately, IT organizations are not populated with only highly technical employees. Many organizations had less-experienced technical personnel implementing and managing open source applications, which created a problem: The products were too difficult to install and use.

As open source spread to less-technical users, problems arose.

To solve these problems, the CD distribution businesses extended the base open source product (again, these were mostly Linux-oriented) with better installation and management mechanisms. With this, these companies moved from being pure packagers of vanilla product to being development organizations in their own right. The additional functionality they created enabled them to generate additional revenues.

Open source businesses extended the base products with better installation and management mechanisms.

IT early adopters not only needed installation help, but also technical support. IT personnel cannot treat product issues in the same manner as hobbyists, with a leisurely attitude toward problems and a curiosity about how they happened. They are under the gun to get systems installed and keep them up and running. IT organizations are used to paying for technical support; indeed, some consider it a prerequisite to using a product. They approached the early open source businesses and requested technical support—and offered to pay. The young open source businesses began to grow on the back of technical support.

Technical support began to be offered as well.

However, an even more compelling reason caused IT organizations to purchase technical support: risk. As open source software migrated into production systems, the potential cost of downtime

Technical support also lowered risk.

became an issue. Open source problems were no longer an inconvenience; they were a business threat. Open source businesses added personnel who could fix bugs as well as offer technical support.

Support services led to training and consulting.

It's a short step from support to training and consulting. The distributors began to offer their expertise to customers looking to jump-start their efforts. The addition of training and consulting allowed these companies to offer a full portfolio of professional services—and allowed users to lower the risks associated with open source.

The common theme of early open source businesses: enthusiasm leading to paid services.

The stories of early open source businesses display a common theme: enthusiasm to help leading morphing into paid services. These businesses have continued to evolve. Several of them have become fairly large companies that do far more than sell standard distributions. They create customized versions of Linux, selecting which portions of the standard Linux modules to include. They also do significant amounts of engineering work, extending their customized Linux versions even further with specialized functionality.

Professional services will continue to be a viable business model.

The professional services business model continues to be viable. The increasing use of open source in IT software infrastructures will raise the demand for technical support and consulting. Entrepreneurs will find many opportunities in open source services. Open source developers themselves might choose to enter the fray; after all, who better to offer support for a product than those who built it?

The New Models: Open Source as a Competitive Advantage

Early business models grew from user/distributor interactions.

The new creation and distribution models of open source laid the foundation for the first two business models. Open source businesses naturally evolved in a rather unplanned manner from the interactions of users and distributors. As open source began to penetrate IT organizations, early open source businesses extended their services to better support this new type of user.

Today, however, new businesses are consciously using open source as an explicit part of their business strategy. These businesses are not run by naïve open source enthusiasts; they are run by technology business veterans who believe significant advantage is possible by incorporating open source into a business plan. To be fair, a number of the early-stage open source companies have long since dropped their breathless enthusiasm and have eagerly considered how to extract more value from their businesses.

New business models based on open source are being developed.

These business strategies are a relatively new development and are the result of entrepreneurs calculating that open source can significantly cut their time to market or reduce the investment needed to create a product. However, it is likely that we are witnessing just the start of this phenomenon; open source will play a role in a significant percentage of startups in the future.

Open source will be a key part of many new technology businesses.

The new business models take advantage of the unique characteristics of open source. Companies can release their product under an open source license to build a large user base very quickly. Distributing their product without licensing restrictions enables them to realize the revenue opportunities possible from a large user base.

These businesses take advantage of the unique characteristics of open source.

Startups also benefit because open source is free. They can create products that incorporate or integrate with open source products. The startup sells a solution consisting of its product along with one or more open source products. The resulting product, incorporating open source software, can be dramatically cheaper than the existing alternatives that require expensive commercial components. Products that were not viable due to price issues are now possible because of free open source software.

Open source's low cost enables less-expensive technology offerings.

Open source
shortens product
time to market.

The ability to incorporate existing open source software illustrates a third reason startups are using open source: time to market. Including existing open source software in a product can dramatically shorten development time and get it to market much faster, which is critical in today's global economy.

The new open source business models can be seen in three different variations. Each of them differs in how it uses open source as part of its business, but each of them fundamentally depends on open source. They are, quite literally, children of open source.

Open Source Add-On Products

One business
model is offering
add-on product to
an existing open
source product.

Some companies have adopted what is referred to as the "Gillette" or "razor" strategy: Give away the razor and charge for the blades. Conceptually, this model seeds a user base with one part of a product distributed at no charge, and then sells additional products that integrate with the free product. For a software product, this might mean something along the lines of distributing a server product at no charge, but selling a management console that makes it much easier to administer. With a large enough user base for the free product, some percentage of the base will purchase the add-on product. For example, if a company can develop a user base of 1 million customers for their open source product, and then get 2 percent of them to purchase an add-on, it will sell 20,000 licenses, which is plenty to build a business on. If the company were to try to sell these licenses without an installed base, it could take years.

The "razor" model
takes advantage of
the digital nature
of software.

This is an especially attractive strategy for a software company, because of the fact that software is a digital product with practically no variable cost. Giving away the base product costs the company virtually nothing, but the potential market from a large user base is significant. Building a large distribution through an open source mechanism enables a company to skip the years-long slog of building a user base.

Extended Open Source Products

Some companies have extended an existing open source product, improving it in some fashion. They then offer their open source–based product for sale, even though it is also available as source to their customers. To date, companies extending Linux are the primary examples of this model. For example, several vendors have created embedded versions of Linux optimized for use in hardware devices. This model differs from the distribution businesses described previously, in that these companies have invested intellectual capital into the baseline product and offer the resulting product for sale. Companies using the extended product purchase it because of the high risk associated with product failures—there is no way to conveniently update an embedded product, so a good relationship with the product developer is critical. Even though the product is free because it is open source, this business model allows companies to realize value by investing in open source development and selling the resulting product.

Another business model is extending an open source product.

EXTENDING LINUX: MONTAVISTA

MontaVista Software, a software company located in Mountain View, California, provides a Linux operating system targeted at embedded uses. For example, Motorola uses MontaVista Linux as the basis for its Smartphone, which provides e-mail and document viewing capabilities along with voice, text messaging, and Internet access.

MontaVista modified a number of aspects of the Linux kernel to make it more suitable for real-time embedded uses. Modifications included power management, POSIX threads, and changing the scheduler. MontaVista's business model included not only an improved Linux, but something just as important to embedded system providers: strong product maintenance and highly responsive support. If you think about it for a moment, a phone provider cannot afford lingering system problems. Any problems have to be addressed *now*. MontaVista addresses this need by selling its improved Linux on a subscription basis, which includes frequent upgrades, patches as needed, and very responsive support.

Interestingly, MontaVista does not attempt to keep its modifications proprietary, but donates them back to the main Linux code base, if possible. This approach stems from their philosophy that their business advantage comes from understanding the embedded systems market and providing a superior price/performance product compared with proprietary operating systems. Linux is the means to an end, not the end itself.

"Appliances" combine hardware and open source software.

A slightly different version of this model is that some companies embed an open source product into a combined hardware/software product—an *appliance*. From the customer's point of view, the fact that the appliance has open source inside is not important; they are purchasing a stand-alone product that provides a particular functionality. For example, organizations that do not want to run mail server software on a general-purpose computer purchase stand-alone e-mail appliances. Even though an open source product (Sendmail) forms the heart of the appliance and is freely available at no charge, the purchasers pay for the convenience of a self-administering appliance.

Hybrid Commercial/Open Source Products

A third business model is offering a dual-license scheme.

A few companies offer their products under two licenses: a traditional proprietary license and an open source license. Products distributed under the first license are offered for sale, whereas the open source version is distributed for free. At first, this seems counterintuitive: Why would someone buy something when it is available at no cost? The answer lies in the implications of open source software licenses.

Open source can "infect" commercial software.

Depending on the type of open source license the product carries, it can require that any software incorporating the open source product becomes open source itself. This is sometimes referred to as the "viral nature" of open source licenses, because using an open source product within another product can "infect" the second product and cause it to become open source.

For those companies that are building a product for sale, this infection is unacceptable. Therefore, they will purchase the product they integrate into their product, even though it is available as open source. By doing so, they protect their product's commercial viability. The companies that create the dual-licensed product recognize that some users of their product must avoid the possibility that the resulting product will become open source. Consequently, these companies release the same product under two different licenses, allowing users to decide what licensing restrictions they want to operate under.

Customers purchase the commercial license to avoid being "infected" by open source.

A NEW OPEN SOURCE BUSINESS MODEL: SLEEPYCAT SOFTWARE'S DUAL LICENSES

Sleepycat Software of Berkeley, California, offers its Berkeley DB database under a dual-licensing scheme. Berkeley DB Data Store is "a high-performance, scalable, embedded data management engine that links directly into the address space of the application that uses it." Berkeley DB is especially well-suited for applications that need data management capabilities but want to avoid the overhead of process switching.

Sleepycat offers Berkeley DB free of charge to anyone who wishes to use it. The download includes source code as well as linkable libraries. However, the open source license requires that if you distribute an application that incorporates Berkeley DB, your product must be open source as well. As a side note, Sleepycat is itself based on open source products from the University of California, Berkeley, and from Harvard University. Their licenses enable commercial products to be created from the original product source code without the resulting products themselves becoming open source. Sleepycat created its product and then released it under both a proprietary licensing scheme and the Sleepycat open source license.

The challenge for many companies needing a product like Berkeley DB is that using it under the open source license would force them to share their intellectual property with everyone in the world. For companies that want to avoid that possibility, Sleepycat sells a different license for the product that allows companies to embed Berkeley DB without turning their product into open source.

If you look at the companies who have purchased Berkeley DB, it's easy to understand why. Sleepycat's customer list includes Cisco, EMC, Google, Motorola, and Sun, among others. None of them could afford to have their intellectual property become open source, so they purchase the non-open source license.

Sleepycat uses the dual-licensing scheme to enable them to run a profitable company while still offering an open source product. Their business model is quite ingenious. Companies can download the product easily and move forward with building their own application. When it comes time to distribute that application, they recognize they must purchase a commercial license or lose their own intellectual property rights. Sleepycat is able to avoid the huge costs that would have accompanied a traditional sales approach—convincing the customer the product is the right one, negotiating a contract, going through a long budget process, and so on—while still ending up with a sale. Sleepycat lets the customer decide the product is right and then realize it needs to purchase a commercial license. It's like stealth selling.

Nearly everyone that first encounters open source software has questions about the software licenses that open source uses. It's important to understand the implications of the license for the software you're using before you get into trouble. The topic of open source licenses is dealt with in Chapter 3, "Open Source Risks."

Business Models: The Bottom Line

The new open source business models continue to evolve.

The different business models are continuing to evolve. Entrepreneurs are creating new business models that take advantage of open source licensing and the market conditions that accompany open source products: widespread distribution, source availability, and an enthusiastic community.

The professional services business model will flourish.

As to the viability of open source–based business models, the jury is still out on how successful the "razor," extended product, and hybrid business models will prove to be. Entrepreneurs are still exploring the economics of software businesses based on products that are freely available—in other words, how they can sell products that are also available for free. On the other hand, the services business model—installation, support, and consulting—based on a freely available open source product is well-established. I expect that it will continue to flourish and that more and more companies will be founded based on existing open source products as those products reach critical mass user communities.

Business models based on open source significantly reduce risk for technology buyers. Over the past few years, mainstream IT shops avoided buying software from small companies because of business risk—the supplier might go bust. No one wants to depend on unsupported software from a defunct company. The business models outlined here protect users because, even if the provider goes out of business, the source is still available. Consequently, buyers can feel more comfortable buying from companies basing their business on open source.

Open source can reduce risk for software users.

In all the discussion of business models it is easy to overlook the central reality of open source: Most open source products are not associated with any commercial entity. Of the more than 80,000 open source products that exist today, fewer than 50 are distributed in any commercial fashion. To succeed with open source, you should be ready to work with software whether it comes from a commercial open source provider or is downloaded directly from SourceForge.

Keep in mind that most open source is not commercially available.

OPEN SOURCE: A "LIQUIDITY EVENT"

A liquidity event is different from a cocktail party! In the parlance of venture capital, a *liquidity event* is realizing the value of a company via an initial public offering or an acquisition. As noted earlier, it is unclear how or whether many of the companies built around open source might ultimately cash out.

However, we can point to at least one company that built a product based on open source and achieved a liquidity event. Here is its story.

Craig Hughes was looking for an antispam product to use on his home Linux system. Searching through SourceForge, he found a number of products; after testing them, he found that the best was SpamAssassin.

It was clear, however, that it wasn't perfect. It needed to run as a server product rather than being executed for each e-mail message. It also needed to be modified to run on Microsoft Windows so that it could integrate with Microsoft Outlook.

Hughes formed a company, Deersoft, to adapt the basic SpamAssassin product to incorporate the needed enhancements. "From the start, we knew that commercial users of the product would want a commercial provider of support. So we started Deersoft to provide product improvements as well as serve as a commercial support provider." Deersoft enabled Hughes and a few employees to support themselves while enhancing the product. Many of those enhancements found their way back to the open source SpamAssassin product.

Spam is one of the two irritants that plague e-mail users. The other, of course, is e-mail viruses. It wasn't long before commercial antivirus vendors recognized that combining antivirus and antispam capabilities into a single product is a natural fit. One of them, Network Associates, then acquired Deersoft to ensure exclusivity for its product line.

Hughes and his partner now work for Network Associates, helping them with their antispam efforts. SpamAssassin continues to be available as an open source product, with many enhancements made by Network Associates engineers incorporated into it.

As this story illustrates, there are ways that open source can lead to business success and even liquidity events. It remains to be seen how many other open source–based businesses also get liquid. As a side note, Deersoft's commercial viability with a SpamAssassin-based product was made possible by the type of open source license SpamAssassin is distributed with. If the product had used a different type of license, Deersoft probably could not have been created. License type makes a big difference. The topic is covered in Chapter 3, "Open Source Risks."

3

Open Source Risks

Executive Summary

Risk represents the probability of something untoward happening in a given situation. Because IT organizations manage the information infrastructure for an entire company, risk is one of the key factors they assess as they make technology decisions. IT organizations are typically very concerned with reducing risk, because computer downtime translates directly into monetary loss.

As IT organizations consider implementing open source solutions, they naturally want to understand what risks they face with this new type of software. The first step toward reducing risk is to understand it. This chapter describes the four major types of risk presented by open source and discusses the methods that are available to mitigate risk. None of the risks are insurmountable, but they should be addressed as part of any open source project.

Licensing Risk

As described earlier in this book, one of the primary ways open source software differs from its commercial counterpart is the licensing mechanism that governs product use and distribution. IT organizations are very experienced in working with commercial software licenses, but are wary of open source licenses. They want to understand what risks they might be exposed to by using open source software. This concern is heightened by the fact that there is a lot of misinformation and FUD (fear, uncertainty, and doubt) floating around the industry about open source licenses. Phrases like "viral licenses" and "redistribution rights" are common in open source discussions. What risk is presented by open source software licenses?

Is risk presented by open source licenses?

What Went Before:
Commercial Software Licenses

Commercial licenses typically restrict rights of usage.

Notwithstanding the fact that every commercial software license is unique (each software company creates its own), they all share a common characteristic: The intellectual property of the product is reserved and held by the creator of the software. Even though you might say, "I bought a piece of software," what you actually paid for was a license to use a copyrighted work of intellectual property. The license comes with a number of restrictions, typically including what machine or machines the product can be used on, who can use the product, and, most important, what right the user might have to pass on the intellectual property to someone else. Commercial software licenses universally share the characteristic that the licensee has no right to redistribute the software to anyone else. Any other party who wishes to use the product needs to contract with the software creator for a license, which usually requires an additional payment.

Open Source Licenses

Open source licenses support rights of usage.

While the deliverable of an open source product is the same as that of a commercial product—software—the license, made possible by the copyright of the product's creators, accompanying an open source product is significantly different. Instead of seeking to limit the redistribution rights that a user has regarding the software product, an open source license encourages redistribution, and even supports it by making the product's source code available. Open source licenses explicitly address what redistribution rights and responsibilities users have.

Open source licenses also impose responsibilities.

The benefits of this type of license have already been discussed earlier in the book and are not addressed here. However, the responsibilities of open source redistribution are important to understand, because this is where most of the confusion about open source licenses originates.

Open source products are typically built with donated labor. The engineers volunteer their time and talent to create a product and make it available for use at no charge. This can raise a problem: What if you take the output of their efforts, slap your name on it, and begin to sell it? Is that fair? If anyone could download an open source product, rename it, and begin to make money from selling it, engineers might be deterred from creating open source products and thereby deprive other users of the benefit of the product. Overall, this would diminish the growth of the open source movement. How can someone be prevented from hijacking others' work product for undesired ends? The answer is straightforward: Use a software license that prevents hijacking.

Open source licenses reduce the possibility of "hijacking" developers' efforts.

It is important to understand, however, that open source engineers do not share a unanimous position about how their work can be used. There is a wide range of opinion about this subject in the open source community. Some members take a very strong—even radical—position that all intellectual property should be available to everyone at no cost. Others accept that the creator of intellectual property should be able to distribute under the conditions he or she desires. A third set of community members aren't too fussy about how their work is used. They create it to be used by anyone who chooses: If someone makes a proprietary product from their work, but thereby gains additional users for it, that's acceptable. As you might expect, this means there are a number of different open source licenses that implement this range of opinions.

Open source developers hold a range of opinions about usage rights.

The type of license a product carries, and its implications, is vital to comprehend before you begin using the product. Just as important is how you intend to use the product. Conditions that might seem onerous could actually be immaterial, depending on your use of the product. The reason for this will be covered in "Asymmetrical License Risk" on page 47.

It is important to understand the implications of the open source license you are using.

Redistribution Responsibilities
of Open Source Licenses

Open source licenses spell out the effect using the product will have.

The purpose of open source is to make software more widely used, and the license that a product carries is designed to encourage that use. How exactly does this work? The license that accompanies the product spells out the conditions under which the product can be used. Most important, the license also spells out the effect of incorporating the open source product into another product, called the resulting product, as it results from use of the open source product.

Open source licenses are a model of clarity.

Incidentally, the licenses themselves are easily comprehensible. They are refreshingly void of any legalese. They describe the implications of using the product in another product. Each license will vary according to how the product's creators wanted it used.

The GNU GPL license is the most "viral" open source license.

The most restrictive open source license is the GNU General Public License (GPL). It requires that any derivative work that incorporates a GPL product must itself be licensed as a GPL product, with its source code available to anyone who requests it. This means that if you use even a tiny bit of GPL code in the source code of another product, the resulting product becomes open source carrying a GPL license. This is sometimes referred to as a *viral license*, because the GPL of one product "infects" a second and makes it GPL, similar to the way a virus organism can insert itself into a human cell and convert it to a virus cell. The key to understanding whether a product has become a GPL product via the "resulting product" mechanism is how the product interacts with the GPL product. For example, Linux is distributed under the GPL license. Any product that includes Linux code will itself become a GPL product. However, products that Linux executes while running (like a commercial database product) are not considered as incorporating Linux and thereby do not become GPL themselves.

A somewhat less restrictive variant of the GPL is the GNU Lesser General Public License (LGPL). The LGPL is designed for products whose creators wish them to become ubiquitous. An obvious example would be a library that offers a standardized way of encrypting data. If this library were used throughout the world, it would enable a broad range of products to interoperate securely. However, if products using the library were to thereby become GPL open source products, many people would be deterred from using it, thereby detracting from its ability to enable interoperability. So the LGPL allows use of the library without imposing the condition that the resulting product becomes open source. Of course, if someone takes the code of the library and incorporates it into a program, that program becomes open source itself. This is a clever license, in that it encourages the use of an open source product without imposing any onerous conditions on the user. Our example product, JBoss, is distributed under the LGPL, which enables an application software company to bundle JBoss without fear that the application itself will thereby become an open source product.

The GNU LGPL license enables widespread use of useful technologies without any "viral" impact.

The least restrictive type of open source license is sometimes referred to as a *Berkeley license,* as a number of open source products emanated from the University of California, Berkeley. This license enables someone to use a Berkeley-licensed product for whatever purpose they desire, including creating a commercial product, without imposing a condition that the resulting product must itself be distributed on an open source basis.

The Berkeley open source license does not impose redistribution requirements.

This discussion makes it seem that there are three different open source licenses. Sadly, this is not the case. There are more than 20 major open source licenses as listed on the Open Source Initiative Web site; however, broadly speaking, they all fall into one of the three types just described.

There are more than 20 different open source licenses.

INFORMATION ABOUT OPEN SOURCE LICENSES

Although the licenses themselves can easily be comprehended by anyone with a college-level education, there are other resources to turn to if you have more questions about open source licenses.

The first is the Open Source Initiative (*www.opensource.org*), which is

a non-profit corporation dedicated to managing and promoting the "Open Source Definition" for the good of the community, specifically through the OSI Certified Open Source Software certification mark and program.

The Open Source Initiative is an advocacy organization for open source and focuses on licensing. It makes a large number of open source licenses available for inspection.

Open Bar (*www.open-bar.org*) is brand new as of this writing. It is a non-profit corporation. A description of the organization:

Open Bar seeks both to educate the non-legal person concerned with his or her rights regarding software development and the rapid rise of technologies using open source and free software, and to serve as a resource for legal professionals advising those in the open source, free software and GPL communities.

Open source (or free) software comprises the fastest growing segment of the software development world. At the same time, it is subject to the widest (and often most incorrect) series of interpretations regarding developers' and distributors' rights. Open Bar seeks to be a resource to educate the public about their rights in this new and somewhat confusing area of law, and to provide sane, non-fee based legal guidance and/or referrals.

A book on open source licenses written by Lawrence Rosen, counsel of the Open Source Initiative, has recently been published. It provides an excellent overview about the general implications of open source software licenses as well as detailed discussions about a number of the more common open source licenses. More information about the book is contained in the bibliography.

These organizations, along with Rosen's book, provide lots of information about open source licenses. If you have more specific questions about a particular situation, a discussion with an intellectual property attorney is probably in order. Be sure that he or she is familiar with open source licensing, as it differs from traditional commercial software licensing.

Asymmetrical License Risk

It certainly seems like open source licenses could be real time bombs. However, the impact of a particular type of license on your organization can vary, depending on how you use the product and what your purpose is for the resulting product. There is asymmetrical risk presented according to your purpose.

Open source software presents asymmetrical license risk.

If you plan to incorporate open source code into a software product intended for redistribution, the impact of the license can be quite profound. For example, if you are a software vendor and use open source code inside of a product that you distribute, it is very possible that your product will thereby become open source itself. This likely means that anyone can request the source for it and then do anything they want with that source, including publishing it, giving it away, or going into competition with you using your own product. Talk about viral!

If you offer commercial products for sale, an open source license can significantly impact your business.

On the other hand, if you plan to use an open source product in your organization with no intent to do any distribution, the risk is quite low. You are not required to make the source of your product available to anyone at all. Indeed, even if you modify the open source product itself, unless you distribute it, you are perfectly free to keep the modified source to yourself, locked within your firewall.

If you do not plan to distribute your resulting product, there is probably very little impact on your business.

Therefore, the risk presented by open source licensing is very asymmetrical. If you are a software vendor, the risk is very high, depending on the type of license used by the open source product you incorporate in your product. If you are a software user, like most IT organizations, you probably don't have much to worry about.

Addressing Open Source License Risk

The primary way to address this risk is to be clear about what use you intend for the resulting product. Without knowing that, there

Be clear about your use of open source software.

is no way to determine your risk exposure. As part of your project plan, be sure to understand your ultimate purpose. The purpose for the product's use should be documented so that everyone remains aware of it; in addition, this topic should be periodically revisited to ensure that the purpose remains the same.

Make sure everyone is aware of the licensing issues of open source.

If you intend to redistribute the resulting product, it is important to make everyone in the organization aware of the license issues in using open source. Well-run software companies have an explicit policy that everyone is made aware of; in addition, they have regular meetings to review any use of open source to ensure that the policy is followed. The policy typically defines a process that must be followed when open source might be incorporated into a product. Topics that are addressed in the process include why the open source product is being considered for inclusion, what type of license it carries, and risks of intellectual property infringement (more on this topic is included in the next section of the chapter).

Including a variety of participants in the discussion of open source is important.

As you might expect, the participants in open source policy committee meetings typically include intellectual property attorneys, as well as technical, marketing, and finance personnel. For technology vendors, using open source means balancing time to market, cost savings, and intellectual property risks. For them, open source is part of a larger buy-versus-build decision.

If you do not plan to redistribute the resulting product, there is probably no need for regular meetings.

For organizations that do not intend to redistribute the resulting product, there is probably no need for regular committee meetings, once the purpose for using the open source has been defined. It's still important to occasionally revisit the purpose discussion to ensure that nothing has changed, but in the absence of a change of purpose, no further work needs to be done.

Security and Quality Risk

Although security and quality risk are not identical, they can be lumped together as they both stem from the risk an organization faces that an open source product might contain source code of which the provenance is not well known. Open source products contain code from many different contributors, and many open source users have questions about the trustworthiness of the source code that results from those contributions.

What is the impact of using a product with many contributors?

Essentially, this risk comes down to whether a user of a software product is safer if all the engineers working on a product are employed by a commercial entity that creates it. The risks that might befall an organization because of problems with a product's source code are the following:

The product might exhibit poor levels of quality. Because there are a large number of engineers who work on an open source product, some of them might not be very good software engineers and would therefore create poor quality code. For example, an individual engineer's contribution might run inefficiently, thereby limiting how scaleable the product is. The problem might be more egregious; the source could have coding errors in it that would cause the product to crash.

Many participants in a project might cause quality problems.

A similar, although slightly different risk, is that the product might be vulnerable to attacks because of security vulnerabilities. These vulnerabilities might be the result of poor quality code or deliberate efforts to make the product fragile. A malicious engineer could insert code that would make the product susceptible to attack.

The product might be vulnerable to attack.

The product might work properly but have dangerous code inserted into it that could cause problems if executed. Often referred to as a Trojan horse, this is the result of an engineer placing code into a

A Trojan horse might be inserted into the code.

product that can be executed at his or her discretion. The engineer might have placed the code in the product to enable him or her to blackmail the user, demanding money and threatening to disrupt the user's business operations if the money is not paid.

There might be a danger of intellectual property infringement.

A risk of a different type is intellectual property infringement. An engineer might place code into an open source product that he or she did not create; rather, someone else created the source. This is akin to stealing and can cause problems for someone using the resulting product. Lawsuits and damages are possible.

What Problems Can Result from Security and Quality Risk?

If there are security and quality problems, the risks are both operational and financial.

The problems that an organization can face from the risks just outlined are both operational and financial. If a product is of poor quality, it will require more attention from operations personnel as it runs inefficiently or even crashes under load. Tracking down quality problems is notoriously difficult because the exhibited symptoms might not seem to be associated with the actual problem. For instance, the symptom could be Web pages that load slowly; the problem might not lie in the pages at all, but might instead be the result of something seemingly unconnected like poorly performing database queries.

Security vulnerabilities expose a company's infrastructure and proprietary data.

Security vulnerabilities can expose an organization to having its infrastructure seriously disrupted and even damaged beyond repair. Proprietary company data could be accessed or stolen, with a concomitant loss of customer confidence. Even worse, there might be no evidence of a security breach; the intruder could passively monitor the system and quietly steal private information. Alternatively, the intruder might take over part of the computer infrastructure, unbeknownst to the organization, and use its computing resources to attack other organizations. Trojan horses might expose the company to blackmail, as the company is threatened with computing problems.

The issue of intellectual property infringement does not typically expose the company operationally—the product is likely to work quite well—but does expose the company to financial risk as well as potentially disruptive legal activities.

Intellectual property infringement exposes a company to legal and financial risk.

How Likely Are These Risks?

It's clear that the consequences of any of the risks just outlined could be horrendous. The company could find that an open source product has wasted a tremendous amount of employee time as well as possibly siphoning off huge amounts of money.

The potential costs of these risks could be quite large.

However, without assessing the probability of these outcomes, it's impossible to tell what a company's actual risk exposure is. Have these risks occurred in the past? If so, how often?

These risks are not confined to open source products. Each of them can occur with commercial software as well. Overall, the level of risk posed because the product is open source is about the same or slightly less than if the product is commercial. The risk might be somewhat lower due to the unique characteristics of open source.

Many of these risks are not unique to open source.

Engineers working on a volunteer basis create open source; they make the product available for inspection by anyone who chooses to examine the source code. It is actually easier to determine the quality level of the product for an open source product because the source code can be reviewed, unlike commercial software products, where source cannot be checked for quality. Furthermore, it is quite easy to determine what level of quality testing has been done for an open source product. Again, this is much more difficult for a commercial product. Overall, it is much easier to assess product quality for open source products. For this reason, product quality

Open source might actually reduce some of these risks.

risks are no greater for open source products than for commercial products, and might even be lower. Much more is said about product quality in Chapter 5, "The Open Source Product."

The risk of malicious code insertion is probably lower with open source.

The risk of someone inserting malicious code into an open source product is certainly present. Because many people have access to the product source, if someone chose to insert Trojan horse code, it could be discovered by someone else examining the code. Furthermore, open source developers work on a product out of personal passion; this makes it unlikely that one of them would want to do something to harm the product with malicious code. Because open source development teams tend to be fairly tight-knit, it is unlikely that someone with malicious motivations would go undiscovered.

The risk of security attacks is probably the same for open source as for commercial software.

Open source is vulnerable to security attacks. The record of commercial software in this respect is not nearly good enough, and open source is not significantly better. This risk is low probability but high cost if an attack does occur. Open source is probably, on average, no better than commercial software products with respect to security attack vulnerability. Every organization should have a security plan in place and apply it to both commercial and open source products; this is the only way that this risk can be mitigated.

The risk of intellectual property infringement is difficult to determine.

The risk of intellectual property infringement is difficult to determine. Because open source developers are not under schedule pressure, and also because they participate in part due to their love of programming, it's difficult to understand why an open source developer would be motivated to place protected intellectual property into his or her product. On the other hand, one attorney interviewed for this chapter said that he was aware of a product into which someone inserted protected code. Source code can be reviewed for an open source product, but just looking at code is unlikely to indicate that it actually belongs to someone else. The only way to truly tell is to compare two pieces of code side by side to see if they are identical. However, in the entire history of software, only a few instances of copyright infringement have been identified, so this is really more of a theoretical risk.

Some projects attempt to deal with this risk by asking the contributing engineers to sign indemnification agreements that protect the project by asking the engineer to agree to defend the project if someone sues for infringement. This may have no practical effect; after all, asking individual contributors to protect the project places the burden on people who are unlikely to have significant financial resources. This doesn't seem like a very likely path forward. In any case, this is all done to protect the ultimate product user, and most product users want to know that the product is safe for use, not that, should it prove unsafe, someone will defend them. Pragmatic IT organizations want operational efficiency, not legal protection.

> Although indemnification is possible, its protection is doubtful.

Each of these risks could be quite dangerous; each of them is actually very unlikely to occur in real-world use. Using open source products does not make them materially more likely; in fact, open source makes some of them somewhat less likely. Depending on the organization's risk tolerance, it might choose to pursue the available options to reduce risk for an open source product.

> Due to these risks, deciding whether to use open source will depend on an organization's risk tolerance.

What About SCO?

At the time of this writing, a flurry of lawsuits and countersuits was flying between SCO, IBM, and others. Essentially, SCO is alleging that intellectual property it owns has been placed into Linux source code without its permission and is suing IBM for infringement. The original suit by SCO has engendered a tremendous amount of ill will in both the open source community and the technology industry at large (leading one commentator to dub SCO the new "most-hated company in technology," dethroning the previous honoree—if that is the correct term—Microsoft). SCO has now extended its legal strategy by bringing suit against some end users of Linux.

This seems to call into question the assertion that there is little risk of intellectual property infringement in open source products. The original suit is wending its way through the U.S. court system with no definitive end in sight. It is impossible to tell what the result of the suits will be, but here are some observations:

None of the attorneys consulted for this chapter believes that SCO will prevail based on the assertions of the suit. Each one of these attorneys specializes in open source licensing issues. Their commonly held opinion is telling.

Corporations have been implementing Linux in increasing numbers during the entire time the suit has been brought. The common wisdom appears to be that the risk of the suit is not that serious.

SCO's current market capitalization is about $150 million. IBM could easily make this problem go away by applying a cash poultice to SCO's wounds. In fact, there has been speculation that SCO brought the original suit to increase its market capitalization and trigger an acquisition.

Finally, and perhaps most important, this suit relates to Linux. More than 80,000 other open source products are completely unaffected by this legal wrangle. As IT organizations begin to adopt other open source products, they can do so without concern for the SCO lawsuit.

Premature Commitment Risk

The ease of using open source can cause risk.

Premature commitments reflect making a choice too early, before all the facts are in. In personal terms, this is the risk of throwing oneself headlong into a relationship before really getting to know the other person. In the context of open source, premature commitment refers to the decision to use an open source product before becoming aware of its strengths and weaknesses as well as failing to determine whether it is the best choice available.

Open source is extremely easy to download and install.

Although calling this risk "premature commitment" might seem flippant, it is a very real problem for IT organizations. Open source can be almost seductively easy to download and begin working with. Someone can go to SourceForge, click a button, and within minutes have a product loaded on a machine. In just a few more minutes he or she can be using the product as part of an application. It's that fast. Why is that a problem?

The primary problem this easy access causes is that of too many products floating around the IT organization. Just as someone can download a product within minutes, someone else can download another the next day. A third person can perform another download the day after that. It is possible to end up with a number of different products being used for similar purposes.

This ease of installation can cause product proliferation.

IT organizations have suffered this problem with commercial products as well. Departments within a company make software selections according to their own requirements, with the result that the company might own a number of different applications all performing the same duty. The very active merger scene during the 1990s caused this problem as well: Each of the merging companies had its own set of applications, so the new entity had two (or more) of everything. In fact, it was much worse than two. One cellular telephone company created as the result of many mergers had more than 50 different billing applications!

The problem of product proliferation is common in IT organizations.

This proliferation of applications caused what you might expect: extremely high IT operational costs. IT staffs had to be larger to keep a full range of application skills on hand. Lack of depth in operations staffs caused delays in problem solving. Companies have moved very aggressively to pare back the number of similar applications they run and manage. Focusing on a smaller number allows them to operate more efficiently.

Product proliferation raises operational costs.

Open source's ease of access can lead to the same issue of application proliferation. Having several different database products, for example, makes it difficult to achieve economies of scale in database administration. Running too many products inevitably raises

Open source product proliferation can raise operational costs as well.

IT operational costs, wasting dollars that could be better spent else-where. At worst, fragmented IT infrastructures can cause morale problems as staff feels they are merely jumping from fire to fire with little sense of accomplishment.

Reducing Open Source Proliferation

It is difficult to reduce the problem of open source product proliferation.

It can be very difficult to address this proliferation risk. Although it is possible to configure firewalls to disallow downloads, doing so creates an atmosphere of mistrust. In any case, this will not solve the problem completely. Employees can download software at home and bring it in to work.

A good approach to this risk is to educate the organization.

A far better approach is to get employees to recognize the issue themselves. By sharing information about the costs of using too many different open source applications, members of the IT organization will recognize the problem and be much more amenable to addressing it. A good first step is to find an opinion leader in the organization—someone whom others look to for guidance on open source issues—and address the issue with him or her. After that, a face-to-face meeting with members of the organization to discuss the problem will create a common understanding of the issue. Some companies, such as Hewlett-Packard, have an open source program office that reviews open source usage to encourage use of common products. It might not be possible to eliminate open source product proliferation, but these steps will mitigate the risk of premature commitment.

Unchanging Process Risk

IT organizations have well-developed processes for commercial software.

IT organizations have had 40 years to hone their processes for selecting, procuring, and implementing commercial software. They have spent hundreds of billions of dollars to optimize their organizations for using commercial software. IT organizations are experts in writing request for proposals (RFPs), negotiating contracts, setting service level agreements (SLAs), managing upgrades, and the like. Each of these tactics is designed to reduce risk—to make the dependence on the vendor manageable. Often IT organizations and their vendors resemble two tired old prizefighters stumbling to the center of the ring to take up the battle where the last round left off. However, IT organizations face a different risk today with respect to open source. It is said that generals always prepare to fight the last war, and thereby leave their nations in danger because their opponent deploys new strategies and tactics. In the same way, IT organizations expose their companies to risk if they expect the same vendor tactics to work with open source products.

We have seen that open source products are created and distributed very differently from their commercial counterparts. New business models are manifesting themselves for open source products, based on different intellectual property rules and much lower revenue expectations. IT organizations must recognize the implications of open source software and develop new methods to select, assess, and implement open source products. Attempting to apply formerly successful processes will leave IT organizations exposed to significant risk, as their expectations about how to succeed with software are left unfulfilled.

> Attempting to apply these processes to open source can cause problems.

There is no magic formula to be applied to open source. Only a thorough assessment of a product, ensuring that all the organization's requirements are addressed, will enable a successful implementation of an open source product. The benefits of doing so are significant: reduced costs, freed-up capital that can be redeployed to better uses, and more flexibility in responding to a world of increasing change. Part II of this book is designed to help your organization realize those benefits.

> These processes need to be modified to enable success with open source.

PART

II

Selecting, Assessing,
and Evaluating
Open Source Software

4

The Open Source
Maturity Model

Executive Summary

This chapter presents the Open Source Maturity Model (OSMM). Mainstream IT organizations demand that software products be complete and mature before they consider putting them into production use. In the past they could rely on commercial software vendors to take responsibility for delivering products of acceptable maturity, but the open source world challenges IT organizations because they must assume responsibility for creating complete products themselves. In contrast to commercial software companies, open source developers typically deliver only one element of the complete product: the software itself. Open source users must locate and evaluate all the other elements that, together with the software, comprise a complete product.

The chapter begins with a discussion about what makes up a complete product, using the very useful analytical framework presented by Geoffrey Moore in his best-selling book, *Crossing the Chasm*. The topic of software maturity is then presented, along with a discussion about why it is the critical quality that must be determined before an open source product is placed into production. Organizations that put off determining a product's maturity until they begin using it will suffer the consequences of their impatience. As a way of assessing the maturity of an open source product, the OSMM closes the chapter. The OSMM provides a framework to determine the maturity level of an open source product; despite the fact that the OSMM is designed to be a quick, inexpensive process, it offers great power to organizations evaluating the production readiness of an open source product.

Of course, presenting an analytical framework in the abstract can be both tedious and unconvincing. To demonstrate the utility of the OSMM, a real assessment is performed in this book for JBoss, a J2EE-compliant application server. JBoss is well-known in the open source community, but is just now gaining acceptance in mainstream IT shops. The book's assessment of the product demonstrates how IT organizations can take advantage of the OSMM in their future open source efforts.

The chapter closes with recommended minimum maturity levels for three types of product use: experimentation, pilot, and production.

The Challenge of the Whole Product

Technology users can be divided into two types: early adopters and pragmatists.

In *Crossing the Chasm*,[1] Geoffrey Moore identified three types of technology users: early adopters, pragmatists, and late adopters. In later works, he further elaborated his model to identify six types of technology users. For our purposes, we can group them into two types of users: early adopters and pragmatists. Early adopters are comfortable using "unfinished" products, whereas pragmatists prefer to wait for the "whole"—or mature—product. Up to now, open source software has been the province of early adopters; today, however, pragmatists are seriously considering open source solutions.

Technology providers must cross the chasm to sell to pragmatists.

Moore wrote his book with an audience of technology vendors in mind. He focused on what they must do to appeal to the different types of technology consumers—in essence, how they could successfully sell to different types of customers. He noted that the shift from selling to early adopters to selling to pragmatists requires a significant change in the product: Moving from an unfinished product to a mature product requires a radically different product (and

---

1.   Moore, Geoffrey, *Crossing the Chasm: Marketing and Selling Technology Products to Mainstream Customers*, HarperBusiness, 1991.

product provider). There is a vast difference between the perspective of an early adopter and that of a pragmatist—so vast, in fact, that it forms a chasm. For a technology vendor to succeed in selling to pragmatists it must be able to cross the chasm.

Open source seems like it would not face this problem; after all, the creators of the product are not focused on selling to any type of customer—early adopter or pragmatist—because the product is free. However, just because no commercial entity exists does not mean that pragmatists don't require mature products, just that someone other than the product developers must take on the responsibility for developing the whole product.

Open source must cross the chasm as well.

To understand how mature products come to exist in the open source world, it is important to understand the differences between early adopters and pragmatists, what makes up a whole product, and why pragmatists desire them so badly.

What are the differences between early adopters and pragmatists?

The Two Types of Technology Users

Early Adopters: Technology Is a Competitive Advantage

Early adopters gain competitive advantage through technology. They believe that innovative technology enables them to develop new product or service offerings or dramatically reduce their cost structure. Technology, if applied cleverly, can change the ground rules of an entire industry to the benefit of the early adopter.

Early adopters seek a competitive advantage through technology.

Examples of early adopters include the following:

Wal-Mart transformed the retail industry through the relentless application of supply chain technology. Its innovative use of inventory tracking, supplier cost assessment, and business intelligence has allowed it to pursue a highly successful strategy of everyday low-cost product offerings. Behind the folksy greeter standing at the store entrance is a company that methodically applies new technology to slash its costs. The company's business strategy, supported by early adoption of technology, has even given rise to a new verb: *Wal-Mart*, as in, "Small town merchants are disappearing because they have been Wal-Marted." Today, Wal-Mart is moving on to the next frontier in supply chain innovation: Radio Frequency Identification (RFID) chips to enable more efficient tracking of inventory.

Charles Schwab shook the investment industry with its original strategy: low-cost stock trading for self-directed investors. The company continued to differentiate itself by offering Web-based stock trading. When that became common to all stockbrokers, Schwab focused on enriching its Web-based product offerings, giving customers a better ability to manage their entire investment strategy via the Web. Schwab also uses technology to reduce its overall cost structure, as it is far cheaper to interact with customers electronically than via telephone sales representatives—in fact, if you call to make a stock trade over the phone, Schwab will have the rep spend time attempting to get you to hang up and place the order via your browser. As of this writing, Schwab is rapidly implementing open source solutions to further reduce its cost structure.

Amazon challenged the book industry by making it possible to use the Web to order books at highly competitive prices. Not only did Amazon use technology to enable online ordering, but also used it to offer services that retail stores couldn't: book recommendations based on previous selections, buying circles describing books most popular with self-selected peer groups, and the ability to speed transactions by storing user details like address and credit card number. Amazon has, of course, gone on to add additional lines of business such as used books, electronics, apparel, and so on. As a side note, Amazon has been a heavy user of open source technology to reduce its IT costs, which makes up a majority of the company's cost structure. Today, Amazon runs its entire computing infrastructure on Linux.

Early adopters track new technologies and begin to use them early in their life cycle. As our examples demonstrate, early adopters apply technology to gain competitive advantage. However, this strategy comes with a price: a willingness to live with the providers of new technologies. New technologies tend to be delivered by small companies, which are passionate, quirky, and organizationally ragged. The technologies these companies deliver often lack complete functionality, might have quality issues, and require users to experiment, endure frustration, and live with product shortcomings. In fact, early adopters can be thought of as finishing schools for immature technology companies, as they highlight product areas that need improvement and help define future development. Early adopters are not concerned that the technology providers are immature companies that don't do a very good job of delivering support, training, or documentation. They are good at living with product shortcomings; in fact, they aren't interested in fully developed technologies, because they don't offer a competitive advantage.

> **Early adopters live with new technology product shortcomings.**

Pragmatists: Technology Offers Efficiency and Cost-Effectiveness

Pragmatists approach IT very differently. They don't seek competitive advantage through technology; they seek efficiency and cost-effectiveness. They can be characterized as "fast followers" who begin implementing a technology once it is successfully applied within their industry. Pragmatists are staffed by employees who expect technology to be easy to understand, fully documented, well supported, and available with excellent training options. These organizations consider a product acceptable to an early adopter as incomplete and will not implement it until it is "finished."

> **Pragmatists want efficient and cost-effective products.**

Pragmatists expect technology to support the company's existing strategy.

It is tempting to deride the fast follower strategy of pragmatists as not very sexy, but that is a mistake. Pragmatists have established business strategies that technology must support. Until the technology is proven and it is clear how it can be applied to the organization's established strategy, it is inefficient to begin using it.

Pragmatists wait for a technology to become proven and then begin to implement it quickly.

Pragmatists begin implementing new technologies once they are proven and complete; otherwise, they risk being left behind by their more aggressive competitors. The primary challenge for fast followers is to determine when a technology is available in full enough form to qualify as a mature product. At that point, fast followers begin implementing these technologies quite rapidly.

Examples of pragmatists include the following:

Target Stores responded to the low-cost challenge of Wal-Mart with its own supply chain strategy. Target offers everyday low pricing on its goods, but also offers promotions on specific goods to drive traffic. Target has applied its technology strategy on a narrower range of goods than Wal-Mart to support its own business strategy.

Merrill Lynch adopted Web technology to support its individual investor business strategy, personal advisors working with investors to mutually create an investment strategy. You can trade stock electronically via the Merrill Lynch Web site, but the company prefers you do so only after you have an established personal relationship with a Merrill Lynch advisor.

Merrill Lynch offers a much broader range of services than does Charles Schwab; whereas Schwab focuses on self-directed individual investors, Merrill Lynch serves individuals, corporations, and governments with a variety of services including stock trading, investment banking, and corporate finance. Although Merrill Lynch uses a pragmatic approach to its individual investor technology decisions, it is very much an early adopter in the rest of its technology decisions. The entire financial services sector is made up of early adopters who use technology to develop new methods of extracting revenues from manipulating financial instruments, and Merrill Lynch is a pioneer in applying technology. It is rapidly implementing open source solutions. See Chapter 9, "Open Source Integration with Other Products," for a description of Merrill Lynch's use of open source.

Barnes and Noble devised a technology strategy that would support its business strategy of selling books both online and in retail locations, a so-called "clicks and mortar" strategy. Barnes and Noble has restricted itself to offering books, music, and video online, but allows online purchases to be returned to its retail stores. It also has a nifty ability to search the inventory of local stores for a specific book, which allows users to see if a book is available locally for immediate purchase.

Pragmatists must understand how new technology will integrate with their existing business strategy before they will seriously consider it. They will not disrupt operations until it is clear how new technology will make them more efficient. Pragmatists focus on the return on investment (ROI) of technology investment and consider every aspect of a technology before a decision is reached.

> Pragmatists focus on ROI and how to integrate new technology into existing operations.

For these organizations, a technology decision must address the following topics

- Product use: Is the product easily understood, easy to configure, and easy to administer?
- Training costs: How much will it cost to get IT personnel ready to use the new technology?
- Support: Who will provide support and how good is it?

- Documentation: How complete is it and how easy to comprehend?

What Technology Users Want
from Their Vendors

Early adopters accept incomplete products.

In Moore's book, he notes that the different types of customers require very different products. Early adopters will accept immature products offering a competitive advantage. They are willing to forego access to sophisticated support, do not insist on high-quality training and documentation, and will even accept a lower-quality product to achieve advantage. Consequently, early adopters are willing to work with small technology suppliers who are engineering-centric, short-staffed, and whose employees are "different," as long as the company provides advanced products.

Pragmatists demand mature products.

Pragmatists, by contrast, demand mature products. Mature products must be of high quality and fully functional, but these factors are just the opening ante for pragmatists. Products also must be accompanied by elements that make them easy to use and efficient to run. Mature products come with a full training program, a sophisticated support operation, well-written documentation, and marketing materials that make it easy to compare the product with its competitors and easy to understand how it fits into a computing infrastructure. Only when all of these elements are present will pragmatists feel comfortable implementing a product.

Pragmatists make up the vast majority of any technology market.

With all these requirements, it's easy to see that selling to pragmatists is a lot more work: it's not enough to deliver the software, you have to deliver it with several other things that take time and money to create. If it's so much work, why do technology vendors choose to sell to this market segment? Because, in the immortal words of the famous criminal Willie Sutton, who, when asked why he robbed banks, replied, "That's where the money is."

In terms of market segment, early adopters represent no more than 15 percent of any technology market, whereas pragmatists make up the remaining 85 percent. If a technology company wants to achieve significant revenues, it must address the product requirements of the pragmatists.

As one might expect, the challenge of moving from a small, engineering-centric company to one with a much larger employee base focused on delivering so many additional product elements is large. Crossing the chasm is the most important challenge any technology company must overcome: The biggest threat to technology companies comes not from their competition, but their inability to morph into a whole product company.

Changing from an early-stage company to a mature company is crossing the chasm.

Because they represent so much of a market, pragmatists dictate to their technology suppliers how they want to do business. Pragmatists patiently wait for the first provider to deliver a product with all the elements they need. When one finally crosses the chasm, pragmatists then begin purchasing the product.

Pragmatists insist that technology suppliers deliver a mature product.

The world of open source, however, turns this process upside down. There are no mature product providers. Waiting for one to cross the chasm is a long, fruitless endeavor. To succeed with open source, pragmatists will have to become much more active and create their own mature product.

However, open source challenges this paradigm.

The Mature Product Dilemma: Pragmatists and Open Source

Chapter 1, "The Source of Open Source," described the world of open source: small groups of committed engineers creating products on a volunteer basis, allowing anyone to download them for free. Open source economics mean that the developers cannot deliver product elements besides the software itself. Other entities

Open source products lack many key product elements pragmatists require.

must provide support, training, documentation, professional services, and the like.

From the technology user point of view, the market is made up of two very distinct communities: early adopters, who thrive on nascent technology, and pragmatists, who require a full array of product elements to begin using a particular technology.

Early adopters are currently using open source.

Early adopters are using open source today in their IT environments. Its low cost, unlimited distribution, and source code availability fit well with a strategy of using technology as a competitive advantage. With open source, early adopters can create new applications very cheaply and focus their IT capital toward other applications. Open source gives early adopters great "bang for the buck."

Pragmatists have not yet begun using open source, but will soon need to.

Pragmatists have been less aggressive about moving to open source. Because they seek to work with established technology providers who can deliver a mature product, they have hung back from implementing open source solutions. Today, however, pragmatists must begin implementing open source solutions like their more aggressive early adopter competitors, lest they be left behind permanently.

Open source presents a mature product dilemma.

This highlights the open source mature product dilemma: a technology provider that, because of the economics of open source, cannot deliver a whole product, and a technology consumer that needs a whole product to begin implementation.

What Is Product Maturity?

Maturity is associated with predictable stages of growth.

As a child grows from infancy to adulthood, he or she becomes more capable and responsible at every stage of life—in short, more mature. Young children learn to walk and talk; older children learn reading and writing; adolescents learn relationship skills and goal setting; adults attain achievements and satisfaction. At each stage, the person can be said to have a certain level of maturity, indicating how well he or she demonstrates the ability to perform the tasks expected at that stage.

Software products go through predictable stages of maturity as well. Early releases of a product provide limited functionality and can be buggy. Subsequent releases provide additional functionality and become more stable. At some point, the product becomes mature enough for production use by pragmatic IT organizations. Software maturity is a concept universally recognized throughout the IT industry, but what are the characteristics of a mature product? In other words, how do we know that a product is mature?

Software products also go through predictable maturity stages.

Mature products provide the following characteristics:

- A feature set that is sufficiently complete that it can be used for real-world business purposes. Early-stage products often lack key functionality that precludes their use in production environments. Conversely, full feature sets do not require pragmatic IT organizations to create workarounds, use additional products to fill in missing functionality, or forfeit critical business functionality.

Maturity means a full feature set.

- A high quality level so that the product rarely fails in production use. Low-quality products require significant administrative work by operations staff, which raises IT costs. In addition, low-quality products can harm a company's business by being unavailable during key business hours.

. . . high quality

- Enough time in the market that longevity concerns about the product are not relevant. Companies often avoid early-stage products because there isn't much experience with them to judge how well they work. Furthermore, using longer-lived products usually (although not always) reduces the risk of an early-stage product provider going out of business.

. . . longevity in market

. . . easy
administration

- Being easy to administer for operations personnel. If a product can be easily configured, managed, and monitored, it can be used efficiently and cost-effectively by IT organizations. Immature products often deliver rudimentary administrative capabilities and offer no integration with popular management tools.

. . . good support

- Support options so that IT infrastructure operations personnel can address product problems in real time. Production systems run around the clock; problems do not confine themselves to a 9-to-5 schedule. If support is not available when it is needed, pragmatic IT organizations are reluctant to use the product. The ability to quickly escalate problems that are causing production problems indicates a mature support infrastructure.

. . . robust
behavior in error
situations.

- Robust behavior when error conditions occur. Immature products often crash when they encounter errors, but products that fail to keep data consistent or are not able to recover state when problems occur are not mature enough for production use.

Beyond these characteristics, you might be able to add one or more of your own. Maturity is a word that captures how "grown up" a product is. It might seem like an imprecise term, but, as a U.S. Supreme Court justice remarked on the difficulty of defining pornography, "I know it when I see it." This is certainly true for product maturity as well. The difference between immature and mature products is obvious when they are contrasted with one another. Anyone who has worked with both can easily identify the differences.

Why Is Maturity Important?

The maturity of a product is key to understanding how well suited a product is for a particular use. Relatively immature products can be used for noncritical systems, whereas production use requires very mature products.

The maturity of a product is important to assess its usefulness.

One of the most important questions an IT organization can ask is, "How mature is this product?" The answer to that question determines if the product will serve its intended use. The failure to assess a product's maturity early enough in the selection process portends dire consequences. Many projects fail when the system doesn't deliver the expected functionality or demonstrates poor performance under production load. The cost of a failed system is high: Beyond the wasted dollars, careers can be harmed, morale ruined, and time to market squandered. In short, failing to ensure that products are mature enough for their intended use can inflict significant organizational pain. Determining the maturity of a product is therefore a critical priority for any IT organization.

Product maturity determines whether it is ready for a given use.

How Does Maturity Impact Open Source?

As discussed earlier in the chapter, open source presents a twist on the usual process of selecting a product. For commercial software products, pragmatic IT organizations expect a single company to deliver the elements required for sufficient maturity: the product, training, support, and so on. If the company does not deliver an element itself, it has recommended providers that will deliver that element at the required level of maturity. For example, Microsoft endorses certain value-added resellers (VARs) as being capable of configuring BizTalk applications. An IT organization can then assess the installation and configuration capabilities of the product as being delivered by a "virtual" single organization: Microsoft and its

Open source presents unique challenges with respect to product maturity.

endorsed VAR. The maturity of the product can be assessed as reflecting the "Microsoft" level of maturity, even though the delivery is by different entities.

Open source product elements are loosely coupled.

In the open source world, the entities that deliver the different elements that make up the complete product are much more loosely coupled. Product elements are delivered by independent entities, with very little control exerted by the development organization. An organization that wishes to assess the maturity of a product must identify how each of the elements will be procured and the level of maturity of each element. This means, for example, that if an organization wishes to assess the maturity of an open source network monitoring product, it must identify where training can be found for the product and how good the training is.

Organizations considering open source must assess product maturity on their own.

Because of the nature of open source development, organizations selecting software cannot expect what they get when selecting commercial software: a sales rep to track down answers to every question, a sales engineer who will perform a demo and perhaps even prototype an application, a support organization to answer questions after the product is installed and running, and so on. Determining the maturity of the product—a vital assessment for the reasons previously outlined—is something the IT organization will need to take on. Open source offers IT organizations much more control of their destiny; it also imposes much more responsibility for their product choices.

Using open source is much like acting as a general contractor.

One way to look at this is to depict the process differently: Rather than procurement from a single provider, it is more akin to creating a coalition of providers to deliver the finished mature product. In the world of open source, selecting software is less like going to a Wal-Mart and more like being a construction general contractor. General contractors draw together independent entities like carpenters, plumbers, electricians, tile setters, and a large number of other contributors. Each member of the project performs his or her task under the guidance of the general contractor, who is responsible for selection and assessment of the people and for the quality of the overall product.

The task for open source users is to identify the needed product elements, assess their maturity, and determine whether the complete product meets the necessary maturity level for the intended use. The challenge is to use a consistent assessment mechanism that ensures nothing is skipped and provides a formal set of assessment criteria. To meet that challenge is the purpose of the OSMM.

The OSMM helps assess product maturity.

The OSMM: An Overview

There are more than 80,000 open source products available for download from SourceForge. Although the vast majority of them are probably not useful for an individual IT organization (or even perhaps *any* IT organization), if even $1/10$ of 1 percent of them are potential candidates for use, that represents a pool of more than 70 products that must be assessed for their maturity for a particular organization.

IT organizations will need to assess many open source products.

Without a formal methodology that implements a standardized analytical framework, organizations are limited in their ability to assess the maturity of a product; furthermore, without such a framework, there is no way to identify the elements of a product that require improvement. Of course, lacking a way to formally assess products, organizations cannot compare open source products to determine which are the best candidates for implementation.

A formal methodology like the OSMM aids the assessment process.

The OSMM assesses a product's maturity in three phases:

- Assess each product element's maturity and assign a maturity score.

- Define a weighting for each element based on the organization's requirements.
- Calculate the product's overall maturity score.

A graphical representation of the OSMM is presented in Figure 4.1. The same figure is printed on the inside cover of the book for ease of use during open source product evaluations.

Phase 1: Assess Element Maturity

The first phase identifies key product elements and assesses the maturity level of each element. Key elements are those that are critical to implementing a product successfully.

The key product elements are as follows:

- Product software
- Support
- Documentation
- Training
- Product integrations
- Professional services

Each element is assessed and assigned a maturity score via a four-step process:

1. Define organizational requirements
2. Locate resources
3. Assess element maturity
4. Assign element maturity score on a scale of 1 to 10

This four-step process is used as the organizational basis for Chapters 5 through 10, which describe the assessment process for each product element.

The first phase identifies key product elements and assesses their maturity.

	Phase 1: Assess Element Maturity			Phase 2	Phase 3
	Define Requirements	Locate Resources	Assess Element Maturity	Assign Element Score	Assign Weighting Factor	Calculate Product Maturity Score
Product Software					
Support					
Documentation					
Training					
Product Integrations					
Professional Services					

Figure 4.1   The Open Source Maturity Model

Define Organizational Requirements

The first step is to define organizational requirements.

The purpose of this step is to define the organization's requirements for a particular element. For example, if an organization wants to implement an open source Web content cache, it must determine what functionality it requires in the software based on the organization's purpose—if it's attempting to reduce bandwidth load, reduce response time, or the like. As another example, if an organization is implementing an open source J2EE application server, its training requirements will be vastly different if it already has significant experience with a commercial application server than if it is beginning to use one for the first time. Defining the requirements for an element is a key step in assessing the usefulness of a product for a particular organization.

Locate Resources

The second step is to locate resources.

Due to the loose coupling of product resources described earlier in the chapter, locating resources for open source products is more complex than it is for comparable commercial products. There probably won't be an "approved partner" list for most products; indeed, there might not be any kind of list. Locating the resources for an element is more challenging, but each chapter offers a number of methods to identify resources that can assist an organization in implementing open source software.

Assess Element Maturity

The third step is to assess element maturity.

This is the key activity in determining how useful a product element will be to the organization. Determining where the element lies on the maturity continuum—from nonexistent to production-ready—lets an organization determine how likely the product will be to satisfy its requirements. Each chapter has a number of guidelines to use in assessing element maturity.

Assign Element Maturity Score

After the maturity assessment is complete, an element maturity score between 0 and 10 is assigned to document how well the product element meets the organization's requirements.

The fourth step is to assign an element maturity score.

The score serves as a concrete outcome of the previous step: It documents the consensus of the organization. Assigning a score also forces the organization to crystallize its judgment. The process of determining the score requires the members of the assessment team to resolve differences in perception, make concrete the reasons for their judgment, and come to a common agreement about the product element.

Assigning an element maturity score documents the consensus of the organization.

Element scores are also helpful when comparing different products—it's easy to compare, say, the training maturity for two different open source content management systems in light of the organization's needs. This can help the organization as a decision tool, enabling it to select one product or another based on the specific requirements of the organization.

The element maturity score makes product comparisons easier.

Finally, the maturity score serves as an input into improving the element's maturity. If a product's overall maturity score is satisfactory, but one element's maturity score is low, the organization can take steps to improve that element's maturity.

The element maturity score identifies areas of needed improvement.

Phase 2: Assign Weighting Factors

The OSMM assigns a weighting to each element's maturity score. Weighting allows each element to reflect its importance to the overall maturity of the product. For example, the heaviest weighting is assigned to the product software, whereas other elements have lower weighting factors to reflect the fact that they are less critical than the software itself in determining overall product maturity.

The OSMM assigns a weighting to each element to reflect its importance.

The default weightings for the elements are shown in Table 4.1.

Table 4.1
Default OSMM
Element Weightings

Element	Weighting
Software	4
Support	2
Documentation	1
Training	1
Integration	1
Professional services	1
Total	10

The weighted score of each element is summed to provide an overall maturity score for the product.

Organizations can choose to adjust the default weightings.

Organizations might choose to adjust the default weighting factors based on their specific needs. For example, if an IT organization is stretched very thin in terms of personnel, it might plan to have an open source product implemented by a professional services firm. In that case, it might increase the weighting factor for professional services to 2 or even 3 to reflect the relative importance of professional services. This allows the OSMM the flexibility to apply to every organization's situation: A product's maturity score will reflect the organization's specific needs and resources.

The weightings must sum to 10 to make the OSMM valid.

The only requirement for adjusting the maturity weighting is that the element scores must sum to 10. Therefore, if the weighting for professional services is increased from 1 to 3, 2 points must be subtracted from the weightings for the other elements. This could be accomplished by reducing the weighting for both documentation and training from 1 to .5, and reducing the weighting for software from 4 to 3. The resulting weighting arrangement for the product is shown in Table 4.2.

Element	Weighting
Software	3
Support	2
Documentation	.5
Training	.5
Integration	1
Professional services	3
Total	10

Table 4.2
Adjusted OSMM
Element Weightings

Phase 3: Calculate the Product's Overall Maturity Score

After each element has been assessed and assigned a weighting factor, the overall product maturity score is calculated. The element scores are summed to give an overall product maturity score on a scale of 1 to 100.

Phase 3 calculates the product's overall maturity.

The Purpose of the OSMM

The purpose of the OSMM is very straightforward: to make a quick assessment of the maturity level of a given open source product. As organizations begin to use more open source products, they will face situations in which there might be several products that fulfill a particular requirement. How can they choose the best candidate? By using the OSMM, the products can be quickly ranked according to their OSMM scores.

The OSMM is designed to make quick assessments of open source product maturity.

The OSMM is designed to enable one or two people to spend no more than three to five days developing an overall maturity score for a product—in other words, a small team can "desk check" a product to see if it is mature enough to be a candidate for an organization's own software infrastructure.

The OSMM enables a small group to complete an assessment in a short time.

The OSMM
identifies
candidates for
further testing in a
pilot
environment.

Of course, no model can completely reflect an individual organization's requirements, nor can a desk check exhaustively assess a product. The purpose of the OSMM is to assess whether a product is good enough for a thorough hands-on assessment, including a test installation and a pilot exercise. There is no substitute for a detailed technical assessment, but identifying the right products to undergo that assessment is a great tool for using open source efficiently.

The OSMM Template

A blank OSMM template is presented in Table 4.3. As you can see by looking at the blank template, the highest possible maturity score is 100.

Table 4.3
Open Source
Maturity Model
Template

Element	Potential Score	Actual Score	Weighting Factor	Element Weighted Score
Software	10		4	40
Support	10		2	20
Documentation	10		1	10
Training	10		1	10
Integration	10		1	10
Professional services	10		1	10
Total product maturity score				100

This template provides a convenient scoring mechanism to be used during a product maturity assessment. Of course, the key to making it a useful tool is the assessment mechanisms used for each element, which are described in subsequent chapters.

A template is
available at the
book's Web site.

A blank template is downloadable at *www.navicasoft.com*. This site also provides blank worksheet templates that organizations can use as they work through assessing product elements.

The site also provides the ability for completed assessments to be uploaded so that they can be shared throughout the open source user community. In this way, IT organizations can leverage work done by others who perform maturity assessments on open source products.

The Web site also serves as a repository of OSMM assessments.

JBoss: A Real-World OSMM Assessment

The succeeding chapters in this book each address one element in the OSMM. Each element is described in the context of how it is delivered for open source products. Several items identified for each element represent successively more mature indicators for that element.

Succeeding chapters address specific product elements.

Without an example, the OSMM might seem rather academic, so a real-world example will be assessed for each element and presented in that chapter. This will allow readers to see how the OSMM can quickly and easily develop a maturity rating for an actual product.

A real-world example is provided in the book.

The example product used in this book is JBoss. For those unfamiliar with JBoss, it is a Java-based, J2EE-compliant application server product. It provides an execution environment for Enterprise Java-Beans with support for server clustering, Web services, and more. JBoss is based on a microkernel architecture, which provides the ability to do fine-grained production administration.

The example product is JBoss.

JBoss is a good example product. It is an open source product that an IT organization would be extremely motivated to assess, because it occupies a key position in software infrastructures. J2EE application servers are, quite literally, the heart of a significant part of today's online transaction processing (OLTP) environments. Any organization considering an open source alternative for this key

JBoss is a good example of how the OSMM can be useful.

piece of software should use any means available to assess the product prior to going live. Therefore, using it as this book's example OSMM provides a good introduction to the thoroughness and effectiveness of the OSMM.

The JBoss OSMM assessment score is available in Table 4.4.

For those who can't stand the suspense of seeing how the JBoss story will turn out in our example, its OSMM assessment score is shown in Table 4.4. Remember, however, that JBoss's score for each product element is contained in the appropriate chapter, and looking at the score without comprehending the rationale behind it shortchanges the meaning of the score itself.

Table 4.4
JBoss Open Source
Maturity Model
Score

Element	Potential Score	Actual Score	Weighting Factor	Element Weighted Score
Software	10	8	4	32
Support	10	8	2	16
Documentation	10	6	1	6
Training	10	8	1	8
Integration	10	10	1	10
Professional services	10	6	1	6
Total product maturity score				78

How to Use the OSMM

The OSMM enables IT organizations to assess open source products.

The OSMM is designed to help IT organizations meet one of the biggest challenges they will face in the next five years: how to productively implement open source software in their computing infrastructure. The OSMM quickly assesses open source products to determine their maturity level. Using it makes the process of evaluating one or more open source products much more efficient.

The OSMM should be applied with judgment.

However, as with every tool, the OSMM can be wielded wisely or foolishly. Applied without judgment, the OSMM will help an organization make a poor decision much more quickly. Applied with judgment, it is a valuable assistant that will help organizations home in on the right choice efficiently and allow them to make much better use of their investments in open source.

The right way to use the OSMM is to assess each product element and assign an element maturity score. After assessing each element, a final overall product maturity score is calculated using element weightings. At that point, the organization has the basis for an informed assessment of the product. It can ask questions such as, "The training on this product seems a little weak; can we live with the available training?" or, "Is the quality level of development high enough for us to feel comfortable running this in a production environment?"

The OSMM enables more informed discussion about an open source product.

If the product comes up short in one or more critical dimensions, the organization can then make an informed choice: The OSMM provides a solid foundation for the decision-making process, but does not take the place of informed evaluation.

The OSMM does not take the place of informed evaluation.

Recommended OSMM Scores

Calculating a score and using it for a decision leaves out one of the most important factors in any decision: its purpose. A maturity score in an abstract consideration is meaningless; what is critical is the maturity score a product needs for a particular use.

The OSMM score should be assessed in light of organizational requirements.

Table 4.5 outlines minimum recommended OSMM scores for use in experimentation, pilot, and production environments. The recommended minimum scores vary according to whether an organization considers itself an early adopter or a pragmatist. Pragmatic organizations are less willing to take risks with software products and therefore require higher maturity scores. In other words, there is an inverse relationship between risk tolerance and required

There are recommended minimum OSMM scores for various organizational uses.

maturity score. Depending on whether your organization is an early adopter or a pragmatist, you should adjust your minimum maturity scores to reflect your risk tolerance, as has been done in the table.

To help you better understand why three different purposes of use are contained in the table, it might help to describe them in more detail.

Experimentation requires relatively low OSMM scores.

The purpose of experimentation is to begin working with a new technology to better understand how it works and what uses might be made of it. For example, many organizations that wanted to begin working with Web services originally began working with open source products. This enabled them to learn the basics of the technology and assess how well Web services would work with their existing infrastructure, without getting a capital budget approved, writing a request for proposal (RFP), listening to endless sales pitches, and so on. There was no intent to place the resulting software into production or even use it as the basis for a pilot, so extensive project documentation, operations training, and the like were not needed. Consequently, rather immature products can be used for experimentation purposes, which is reflected in the low recommended minimum scores.

Pilot projects replicate production environments and require higher OSMM scores.

Pilot projects serve the same purpose as out-of-town productions of Broadway plays. They seek to replicate the conditions that a product will operate in under production loads, but they are primarily oriented toward learning how everything about the product works and to ensure that all elements of the product exist and are operational. Just as out-of-town productions enable adjustments to be made before the all-important opening night, pilot projects enable shortcomings in any aspect of a product to be identified and fixed before the all-important go-live date.

Production carries a simple meaning: The business relies on the product working correctly in all aspects. All the necessary functionality must be present, people trained, operational procedures defined, and necessary support mechanisms ready. When a new application goes into production, it's too late to find out that the people running it don't know how to back it up properly.

Production requires the highest OSMM scores.

With these descriptions, it's easy to understand that, as the use of the product reflects more production-like needs, the necessary maturity score will need to be higher. The recommended minimum scores contained in Table 4.5 reflect that fact, and offer appropriate guidance for organizations performing OSMM assessments on open source products.

Recommended minimum OSMM scores are contained in Table 4.5.

It must be emphasized, of course, that the recommended minimum scores are just that: recommendations. You might choose to use a product even though it fails to achieve the recommended minimum score for your purpose. In fact, you might decide that your organization would like to use different values for the minimum scores. The purpose of the recommendations is to provide a good starting point for determining how mature a product needs to be for a given purpose. If you feel a different value makes more sense for you, that's perfectly fine. It's more important that you perform a maturity assessment and determine what your minimum acceptable score is than to adhere rigidly to recommendations that might not reflect your needs.

You can adjust OSMM recommended scores to serve your unique organizational needs.

Purpose of Use	Type of User	
	Early Adopter	**Pragmatist**
Experimentation	25	40
Pilot	40	60
Production	60	70

Table 4.5
Recommended Minimum OSMM Scores

5

The Open Source Product

Executive Summary

With this chapter, we begin assessing the individual elements of the complete open source product—and we begin with the most critical element of all, the code itself. Source code forms the core of the entire product, so it makes sense to begin the assessment process there.

One of the great benefits of the open source product is the availability of the source code itself. In assessing commercial software, the product's functionality can be determined by looking at the product description. The quality of the product can be appraised by performing testing routines developed to exercise the product. That would be about the limit of one's ability to assess the product and its quality.

By contrast, open source products offer much more transparency, making a much more thorough assessment possible. Source code availability enables an examination and evaluation of the quality of the code itself. The extent and quality of the quality assurance (QA) process can also be determined for an open source product.

Beyond the code itself, most open source engineers are available for direct interaction regarding the product. They are typically very accessible for discussions that can help in evaluating the product.

Of course, before you can determine how well a product fulfills an organization's needs, you need to understand what those needs actually are. After all, you can't take a measurement without a yardstick to measure by!

This chapter outlines four different aspects of an open source product that should be evaluated:

- Functionality
- Quality of the product
- Longevity of the product
- Quality of the engineering team

The chapter ends with an assessment of our example OSMM product, JBoss. A checklist that covers each of the evaluation areas for JBoss is included (see Table 5.3 on page 120). This offers an example of how your organization would move through a product assessment process, capturing relevant data about the product. Based on the information noted on the checklist, a point assignment for the product portion of the OSMM has been made. Again, this offers an example of how other products can be rated for product maturity.

Assessing Product Maturity: The Process

As outlined in the previous chapter, assessing the maturity of a product element is a four-step process:

1. Define organizational requirements
2. Locate resources
3. Assess element maturity
4. Assign element maturity score on a scale of 1 to 10

Defining Organizational Requirements

The first task is documenting the required functionality.

The first task in assessing a software product is to document the functionality that it must deliver. Unfortunately, too many times this part of the assessment process is cut short or not undertaken at all. It's easy to conclude, "We don't have enough time to develop detailed specifications. We need to choose *now*!" This approach to specification is captured in the rhetorical question, "Why is there never enough time to do it right, but always enough time to do it over?" A clear set of product requirements is the key to open source success.

Therefore, the right first task is to document the product requirements: What does the product need to do? Even though it's the right first task, and a necessary precursor for success, it isn't easy, which is why it's often shortchanged.

This step is often shortchanged.

This book does not focus on requirements generation—there are a number of good books on the subject and even software products that assist in requirements definition (including, naturally, a couple of open source products). However, there are some aspects to consider that are specific to open source.

There are some aspects unique to open source.

Put Together a Requirements Task Force

Because open source is a different animal from commercial software, it is often easy to assume organizational processes that work fine for commercial software will work for open source as well. For example, the organization's procedures might assume there will be a physical deliverable for the product, which is very unusual in the open source world. One of the great benefits of pulling together a task force is that not only will product requirements be sent upstream, but information will also flow downstream to groups that will be affected by the product. This task force should include personnel that are rarely part of the IT decision-making process. For example, it might be important to include an attorney as part of the group to ensure that the license type of the product is acceptable to the organization. Because open source differs so much from its commercial counterparts, it's wise to form a broad-based task force to ensure that every group that will be affected by the product is involved in the selection.

Create a requirements task force.

Identify the Functional
Requirements for the Product

The marketing
materials for
comparable
commercial
products help
identify necessary
functionality.

This can be a bit tricky for open source products. Trying to determine the functionality that the product must deliver isn't always easy. Commercial software firms have marketing departments that churn out material describing the company's product, how well it maps to the appropriate standards, how it differs (always better) from the competition, and so forth. These marketing materials can be a great help in outlining product requirements. By bragging about the product, these materials help identify the functionality that the organization needs.

Open source
products usually
lack such
marketing
materials.

Open source typically lacks the equivalent outreach capability. There might be a brief, laconic description of the product's functionality on the project home page, but there will be no comparison charts, discussion of the "product space," or the like. Nevertheless, here are some ways that functional requirements can be put together for open source products.

Review Any Applicable Standards

Standards can be a
useful source of
product
requirements.

Open source products often implement a formal or de facto standard. If the project home page identifies one or more standards that the product implements, the standard(s) can be a good starting place for the requirements definition. Determine what state the standard is in (draft, comment, etc.) and list it as a requirement.

Review the Functionality the
Commercial Vendors Implement

Review the
functionality of
corresponding
commercial
products.

Take advantage of the materials churned out by the commercial vendors that offer similar functionality. They will often provide detailed lists of their product functionality, which can offer an excellent starting point for a requirements matrix.

See if "Best-of-Breed" Requirements Have Been Created by Analyst Organizations

The only organizations more skilled than vendor marketing departments at churning out market segmentations, functionality definitions, and the like are the technology analyst organizations. They often create product matrices that list functional requirements for a particular type of product. If an analyst functionality matrix is available for the product to be assessed, it can help identify functional requirements.

See if analyst organizations have created functionality matrices.

Poll Your User Community

One of the benefits of putting together a broad-based requirements task force is the ability to poll members about their product requirements. These might be functionality requirements, but there can be process requirements as well. For example, the help desk might require that documentation be available in printed format, which would need to be documented as a product requirement. Certainly operations might have expectations about how the product should work and information it should make available for monitoring purposes. It's not always easy to get people to sit down and document their product expectations, but the effort is definitely worthwhile, as it can avoid significant problems later on.

Poll the user community.

Document the Functional Requirements

Once the process of developing requirements is finished, be sure that a full list of functional requirements is created and made available. This is critical so that an open source product's capability can be mapped against the list, but also because it provides an ongoing formal definition of what the product is expected to do. This can be very useful, because as new individuals or groups get involved in the assessment and selection process, they can quickly get up to speed on the requirements by checking the documentation. A secondary benefit of documenting the requirements is that it allows for ongoing review, which might add requirements not identified earlier.

Be sure to document your organization's product functionality requirements.

Locating Resources

The next step is to locate product candidates.

Once the functionality requirements have been defined, the next step is to identify one or more open source candidates. This can be a very challenging task because open source projects typically are not able to mount a marketing program to make potential users aware of the product's existence and capabilities. The free, anonymous nature of open source makes it much more difficult to easily identify products that you would consider—if you only knew about them. Consequently, this requires you to take a more active role in seeking out candidate products. This might seem like a challenge, but here are some techniques to help you create the right candidate pool of products for your maturity assessment.

Search Open Source Project Portals

Search open source project portals.

The first technique is to go to the main repository of open source projects: SourceForge. SourceForge has two ways to search for products. The first is a hierarchical listing of projects organized according to a technical taxonomy. For example, the first three types at the highest level are communications, database, and desktop environment. The list can be traversed to find potential products.

The portals support textual searching.

A second method of finding projects in SourceForge is to do a textual search. Entering one or more words in the search field will bring back a list of projects that use those word(s) in their descriptions.

Even projects that are not hosted in SourceForge will often have a description page available so that searches will select these products as well.

Search the Web

Web searches can locate candidate products.

A second technique to help you create your product short list is to search the Web using search engines. Web search engines can be very useful in identifying potential products that meet your needs.

Furthermore, the returned links will often link to pages that are about products, rather than the product pages themselves. These can be very useful as they form a way to interact with a user community focused on the same area on which your organization is focusing. One of the themes of open source is to take advantage of others' experiences rather than reinventing the wheel; finding information about specific open source products or about the general area from the user community can be a great benefit in locating candidate products. The best way to take advantage of search engines is to search on words that identify the key functionality you require in the product. For example, a search that would turn up our OSMM example, JBoss, would contain the words J2EE, application server, and open source. The first link when these terms are entered into Google leads to JBoss.

Ask Open Source Developers

Open source developers are often very aware of the existence of open source products that might be appropriate for a given use. This is particularly true for developers who have created a product that is a potential candidate. Querying open source developers about potential products is another technique to create a product candidate pool. It's easy to interact with these developers via e-mail—and, unlike the commercial software field, there is less need for them to make their product look better by criticizing another. Generally, open source developers are very willing to help identify potential candidate products and very astute about what products might be worth considering.

Open source developers can recommend products.

Post to Mailing Lists

There might be a mailing list devoted to the product area for which a candidate pool is being created, or there might be a mailing list that is complementary. For example, if a network management tool is being sought and the organization would like to use Linux as the operating platform, a post to an appropriate Linux mailing list will

Open source mailing lists can be polled for recommendations.

generate some candidate products as well as some opinions about them. More information about mailing lists, including how to find them, is contained in Chapter 6, "Open Source Technical Support."

Ask Vendors

Commercial vendors might be able to recommend products as well.

If a commercially purchased product is involved in the overall application infrastructure, the provider of the product might have some insights about potential product candidates. As in the example identified earlier, if the chosen platform is Linux and the organization has a relationship with a Linux provider, the provider could be questioned to see if they are aware of potential product candidates.

This option is probably available only to fairly large IT organizations that have the ear of a platform provider. If this is an option, however, you should definitely take advantage of it.

Put Together a Candidate List

Pull together a short list of candidates.

From the five techniques just described, a list of potential product candidates can be put together. It might list many candidate products. If there are a number of candidates, rank them to create a prioritized list for investigation purposes. Although the OSMM is designed to efficiently identify good open source product choices for an organization, too many candidates can overwhelm even an efficient process. A good rule of thumb is that a short list of no more than three to five candidates for further assessment should be the outcome of this step in the process.

Look to the user community for help in creating a short list.

In terms of the actual list, several factors should help create the product ranking. If a product has been mentioned several times, it is a good bet for more detailed examination. One of the strong indicators of a product's maturity is the size of the user community. Evidence of a sizable user community, even in something seemingly inconsequential like number of mentions in the process of candidate list creation, can help identify a high-priority candidate product.

Recommendations received as a result of polling users should definitely influence whether a product is put onto the short list. Feedback from users is extremely valuable, as they will share the same perspective as you: a concern with how the product actually works in production environments. Actual users are best qualified to judge the attributes of the product. Of course, you need to keep the feedback in perspective. Postings in public forums are often not censored or even screened, so they should be judged on their quality. Someone with an axe to grind might post a strongly worded opinion (or a rant, as they are often described), which might say more about the poster than the topic of the posting. In general, postings provide an excellent insight into the experiences of product users, so they are a good method to help develop the candidate short list.

Keep user recommendations in perspective.

The quality of interaction with the product developers (if there has been any) should be a factor as well. Selecting an open source product is, in part, selecting a development team, so the ease (or difficulty) of establishing rapport with them should strongly influence whether the product makes the short list.

Quality of interaction with the development team is important.

At this point, the organization should have a rank-ordered short list of products to investigate further. The right product to meet the functional requirements developed at the beginning of the process should be one of the products on this list. The next step is to begin a detailed assessment of how well each of the candidate products fulfills the product requirements.

The outcome of this step is a rank-ordered short list.

HOW OPEN SOURCE PROJECTS GET STARTED: SAMBA

This chapter is all about assessing a product's maturity level. It assumes a product with a download site, feature description, and development team—in other words, a well-established product. What about the other end of the maturity spectrum? How do open source projects get started?

In the open source community there's a saying that open source projects are started by people who are "scratching an itch," meaning that they create a product to solve a problem they're facing, which they then make available to others who have the same problem.

Samba is a good example of this. For those not familiar with Samba, it is an open source product suite that provides seamless file and print services to clients—it enables Windows and Macintosh clients to take advantage of Linux (and other operating system) file systems and print services. Samba is one of the most popular open source products, with several million cumulative downloads.

Samba grew from a two-person project started by Jeremy Allison and Andrew Tridgell. Allison recounted the following as the genesis of the project:

> It started in the early '90s when a software company I was working at was dissatisfied with a commercial product that networked Windows clients and UNIX servers. It had terrible performance and crashed all the time, not to mention being extremely expensive.
>
> In my spare time I got a spec from Microsoft about how the Microsoft file system worked and built, along with Andrew, a product to allow Windows boxes to use the UNIX-based source code management system. I was able to get the company's support to work on it because it saved us a lot of money on the licenses for the product we had been using. We just kept working on it, improving it, and released it so others could use it as well. Today, it's taken on a life of its own.

Samba is now used throughout the globe, with more than 20 mirror sites located in other countries. It offers many more features than the original product that Allison and Tridgell developed, and has a significantly larger development team (approximately 20 engineers). It's not easy to see Samba's origins in the current product, but it started as a way to ship source code files to a central server—an itch that needed to be scratched.

Assessing the Functionality
of the Product

The first and most important step in assessing a product is to determine if it offers the necessary functionality. Does it do what you need it to? If it fails to, it doesn't matter how mature its other elements are; that's irrelevant. The product has to deliver the right functionality. Therefore, the first task in any product assessment is to evaluate how well its functionality matches your organization's requirements.

Assuming that the organization has created a functionality requirements definition, as outlined at the beginning of this chapter, how can it assess how well the product in question meets those requirements?

Before starting the functionality assessment process, you should keep several things in mind:

- No product will completely meet the ideal functionality specification. The requirements gathering phase identifies a "wish list" of every person's (or organization's) desires. Just as actual individuals always fall short of one's ideal romantic partner, actual software products never deliver ideal functionality. Likewise, just as personal shortcomings don't keep us from establishing relationships, functionality shortcomings shouldn't keep us from making a software decision. Failing to choose is a decision itself, one that can have consequences as severe as making the wrong choice. Don't drop a product just because it isn't perfect.
- Software is a plastic medium. Every software product (at least those not in senescence) is evolving and improving. The functionality available in the current release is not the endpoint for the product. Even if a candidate product has

The first step in assessment is to match the product to your organization's functionality requirements.

How can that assessment be done?

significant functionality shortcomings, it might not in the
future, so a product should not be rejected out of hand
because it does not fully meet the organization's
requirements. Because of the source availability of open
source, there are ways to mitigate missing functionality in an
otherwise good choice.

- As a by-product of the last item, rather than using a yea-or-
nay judgment on the issue of product functionality, a better
method is to take into account the extent to which a product
fulfills an organization's requirements. A product that is
missing only one or two features might be considered very
acceptable, whereas one that is missing many functionality
requirements would be considered a very poor match for the
organization's requirements. Of course, if a product is such a
poor match for the functionality requirements, it probably
doesn't belong on the short list and should be dropped before
further work is undertaken.

Assess the Product
Based on Its Description

Begin with the product description.

Begin the functionality assessment with the product description. As
described earlier in the chapter, every open source product has a
home page that provides a high-level presentation of the product's
functionality. It usually will not describe the product with enough
granularity to do a detailed comparison with your functionality
requirements, but it is a good place to start.

Reference applicable product standards.

If the product implements a standard, it will usually reference
the standard and perhaps the level of adherence to the standards.
Standards are notoriously changeable until finally approved and
many times a product will implement an interim version of the
standard. In any case, a standard (no matter what point it is at
in the approval process) is a good point of comparison with the
product requirements.

Query the Developers

Because the project home page usually does not contain enough information about the product, the next step in establishing whether a specific required functionality is available in a product is to query the developers. A real benefit of the open source world is the ability to interact directly with the development team to ask questions about the product.

Query the product developers.

The open source world does not tolerate fools, so efficient interaction with the developers is critical. Rather than sending an e-mail with a question like "What does your product do?," a better approach is to identify the functionality about which more information is required, and ask specific questions about it. For example, rather than asking "Do you support XML input?," a better, more specific question would be "Do you have a description of the XML input you support and are there any examples to look at?"

Be sure your queries are to the point.

Developers of open source products are usually very accessible and available to answer questions. This can be an excellent way to gather detailed information about how well the product implements the required functionality; take advantage of it. This process can also form a relationship with the development team that can have huge benefits throughout the lifetime of product use, so it is a valuable part of the requirements phase.

This process can also help form a relationship with the development team.

Query the User Community

Another good source of information regarding the product's functionality is the user community itself. Just as the developers are usually accessible, members of the user community are typically amenable to sharing their experiences with a product.

The user community can help assess product functionality.

There are several ways to locate members of the user community:

- If the open source product has its own Web site, it will often list organizations that use the product. Contact someone from the companies listed and ask about their experiences with the product. They can also be questioned to see if they have specific information about functionality that is part of the selection criteria.
- The mailing list for the product offers two valuable ways to assess the product's functionality. First, the archives can be searched to see if someone has addressed the aspects of the product you are interested in. Someone else might have asked whether particular functionality is available and that discussion can be useful in the functionality assessment phase. Second, it is possible to query individuals who have posted on a topic similar to what you are interested in. They can give you detailed information about specific functionality that is valuable for your assessment purposes.
- A third method of locating members of the user community is via Web searches. Often, someone will have created a page or posted onto a Web site information related to the product. By examining these postings, it is possible to benefit from their experience with the product.

User community queries should be to the point as well.

The same informal rules of engagement that are presented in the section on interacting with the developers of the product also apply to members of the user community. People are usually delighted to share their experience with a product, but don't want to feel taken advantage of or abused. Focused questions can mine a rich vein of knowledge, but questions that seem too general or lazy will probably be met with an abrupt dismissal. Respect the knowledge of the user community and don't abuse it.

Assessing Product Longevity

A key indicator of product maturity is how long it has been around. Products that have been available for long periods of time tend to be more mature. Early releases of products are notoriously buggy, reflecting the fact that the products are used (and misused) in ways the developers never imagined. These uses of a product exercise it in ways that the developers never anticipated; product weaknesses are exposed in real-world use that did not manifest during development and testing. In essence, the product is stressed by being exposed to the real world and that stress turns up bugs that need to be fixed before the product is ready for production environments. This process plays itself out over the first few releases of a commercial product; wise users seek to avoid the problems associated with early product releases. The importance of product longevity being a good maturity indicator is captured in the IT cliché, "Never use a 1.0 product."

Product longevity is a key product maturity indicator.

Although the preceding statement makes light of the poor quality of early versions of products, it highlights the importance of determining the longevity of a product as part of the assessment process. Simply put, the longer a product has been around, the more mature it is.

The longer a product has existed, the more mature it typically is.

As you might expect, it is not as simple to determine an open source product's longevity. The rule of thumb that works for commercial products—see how high the version number is ("The higher, the more mature, and, by the way, avoid 1.0 products")—doesn't apply very well to open source products.

Assessing open source product longevity can be a challenge.

Open source developers have a different philosophy about product versioning. It is an article of faith in the open source community that the widespread availability of products early in their development cycle quickly identifies bugs and improves product quality.

Open source versioning differs from its commercial counterparts.

This belief is reflected in the open source truism, "Many eyes make all bugs shallow." Consequently, there is little belief in the open source community that early version numbers are correlated with poor quality.

Open source products avoid feature bloat.

Another difference between the open source world and the commercial software world is that there is far less pressure to implement features as part of market competition. In commercial software, release numbers are often raised to indicate new functionality. Open source developers believe that this competitive process often leads to unnecessary features put into products purely for bragging rights rather than for utility reasons. It is described as "feature bloat," and open source developers are proud that this kind of thing is absent from open source products. Again, the implication is that higher version numbers are not necessary.

A real-world example of longevity assessment.

To give a real-world example, my firm recently developed a system for a client based on Web services. A Web site captured subscriber data, which then needed to be inserted into a subscriber database located in a remote data center. We proposed using a Web services communication mechanism and MySQL as the data repository. Part of our process was to identify and assess the open source options available for the different parts of the system. Although the MySQL database carries a version number of 4.0.13, which would satisfy the traditional measure of longevity, our choice for the Web services piece of the application was the Perl module SOAP::Lite. It carries a version number of .55, which would not even pass the 1.0 test! We needed a different way to assess its maturity to understand if it would be serviceable for our client's needs.

For the purposes of assessing open source longevity, the following measures are good proxies for the traditional version number assessment:

- The version number of the product. Although the version number must be interpreted, it's a valuable indicator as to product longevity.
- The life span of the product. This information is easily available on the SourceForge product home page. This gives an idea of how long it has been around.
- The total number of downloads. Although this does not exactly address longevity, it does give a good sense of the size of the user community, which grows in step with the length of time a product has been available. Something to keep in mind is that a high percentage of downloads are done for research purposes and the actual number of downloads that are in use will be smaller. A good rule of thumb is that perhaps 10 or 20 percent of downloads are destined for actual product use.

For our assessment of SOAP::Lite, we identified each of these items, as shown in Table 5.1.

Version number	.55
Life span	October 2002
Total number of downloads	The primary download location for SOAP::Lite is *www.cpan.org*; CPAN does not track total number of downloads. SOAP::Lite is also available for SourceForge, which has had 1,888 downloads to date.

Table 5.1
Soap::Lite Longevity
Assessment

Looking at these statistics, one might conclude that SOAP::Lite has poor longevity. However, we took some other aspects of the product into account in examining its longevity:

- Web services is a nascent technology. It has not been available that long, so products implementing Web services would not have an extended life span. Also, Web services is a "hot" technology, so that would tend to allay some concerns about the future longevity of this product. SOAP::Lite is the most established Perl module implementing Web services, so it is probably going to be a survivor.

- A book on SOAP::Lite was recently published. Without going too much into the topic of documentation, which is discussed in Chapter 7, "Open Source Documentation," the availability of commercial documentation is a powerful indicator of product maturity. The book has sold approximately 1,700 copies to date, indicating a user base of at least 17,000.

Based on these factors, we assigned SOAP::Lite a longevity score of 5. This might seem low, but the overall maturity score of the product was sufficient for us to feel confident about its maturity.

Determining the Level of the Product's Longevity

One valuable way of assessing product longevity is to compare it to another product.

The caveats listed earlier pertaining to judgment also apply to the longevity factor. It is perhaps easier to rate a product's longevity when it is being compared with one or more products. If one product has been available for 8 months, whereas another has been available for 36 months, it is easy to see that the second product would deserve a significantly higher longevity score.

However, using the factors of version number, life span, and total number of downloads establishes a rough judgment of longevity.

Assessing Product Quality

Software quality is a key to product maturity.

Quality is a key factor in determining a product's maturity level. When assessed too late in a project life cycle, lack of quality can have disastrous consequences. Quality is inversely related to risk: The higher the quality level of a product, the lower the risk that it will fail in use, causing production outages and raising costs. Good IT organizations pay attention to risk factors and seek to reduce their overall risk exposure.

Because of the opaque nature of commercial software companies it is very difficult to determine the quality level of their products. By opaque, I refer to the fact that commercial software companies shield their development teams. They do not want engineers bothered or diverted by customer inquiries. They also want to ensure that their staff is not subject to headhunting raids. Some companies might not want potential customers to know how much (or how little) manpower is actually devoted to the product in question.

> Commercial software quality levels are typically difficult to determine.

With respect to quality, this opacity means that there is no easy way to determine the level of a product's quality effort. The size of the QA team cannot be ascertained. The thoroughness of testing is undisclosed. There are really only two methods to assess the quality of a commercial software product: a pilot implementation of the product to see how well it performs, and assessing rumors that float around the industry. Neither of these methods is very satisfactory and neither of them really help to reduce risk.

> Many of the factors affecting commercial software quality are opaque.

A real strength of the open source world is that there is much more quality-related information available about a product. There is much more transparency of information, which enables IT organizations to quickly and cheaply assess the quality level of a product. This transparency assists an organization in reducing the risk associated with using a product.

> Open source quality factors are much more transparent.

It's important to remember that quality refers to far more than just the testing that has gone on for a product. Although important, testing is only one aspect of a product's quality. Other factors like the quality of the source and the level of check-in activity affect quality and should also be examined. Fortunately, open source's transparency enables all of these factors to be evaluated. A number of techniques are available for your organization to examine the overall quality of an open source product.

> Quality is much more than just testing.

Examine the Source Code

Source code examination is one way to assess quality.

The availability of product source code defines the term open source. It is easy to access the source for whatever purpose an organization desires, including assessing the product's quality. One method of quality assessment is examining the product's source code.

Consistency of coding style can be assessed.

Reading source code offers the opportunity to assess the quality of the product's engineering. The code can be examined for consistency of style, which, strictly speaking, does not determine how well the product operates. However, consistent coding style does make product maintenance easier. If an organization is considering making its own code contributions to a product, it will want to adhere to the coding standards in place. Even if the organization does not plan to add code to a product, looking at how consistent the code is throughout the product offers an insight into how well the development team coordinates its work.

Examine code to see if the development team uses best practices.

The purposes of examining source code are to determine how well the developers follow industry best practices in their work and to make an assessment of the quality of the developers' skills. The subject of code inspection cannot be covered in detail in this book; however, the key aspects of product quality that a code inspection will address are as follows:

- Whether a consistent coding style is used throughout the product source base. Consistent style makes source code easier to maintain and reflects good communication among development team members. Even if an organization does not intend to work with the product source code, it will rely on others being able to effectively work with the source, so a high-quality source code base is a good indicator of product quality. The best way to determine this is to select portions of the code at random and compare them for consistency.

- Whether the code is written in a clear, maintainable manner. Software engineers often attempt to exhibit cleverness in how compactly they can write code, but this can be achieved at the expense of code comprehensibility. Good coding practice focuses on making code easily understood. The presence of comments that describe what the code is doing is also a good sign. Clear, easily understood code is critical for open source products, because there is less control on who can modify the source. Therefore, the code should be written so that people who might not be intimately familiar with the product and its history find it easy to understand.

- Whether key sections of the code are well written. If an organization is planning to modify or extend the source, it should pay particular attention to the portions of the product that will be changed. If those sections of the code base are poorly written or documented, it will be far more difficult to make changes to the product. Ideally, the individual or group who will be making the changes should be part of the inspection team.

It might be that the organization does not employ anyone experienced enough in the product's language to make an assessment of code quality. In that case, someone with that level of experience should be located and employed on a contract basis to do an assessment of the code quality.

If the organization does not have an expert on staff, use an outside resource.

Evaluate the QA Effort

The cliché about software engineers is they love to program and hate to test. Like many clichés, there is more than a little truth in this statement. The QA function originally came into existence because development organizations needed someone to make sure the product functioned properly. QA groups develop test plans that describe the test strategy for a project and then develop test suites

QA ensures that the product functions properly.

to implement the test strategy. The test suites are typically run against each release of the software to assess its quality level.

QA did not always ensure complete functionality testing, however.

The use of QA organizations to test the product led to other problems, however. With quality a downstream activity, projects took longer because of multiple round trips between engineering and QA to get the product up to scratch. There is some evidence that products ended up being tuned to meet the test suite developed by the QA organization at the expense of overall product quality. The worst problem with this approach is that it lets developers avoid responsibility for the quality of their work because quality is "the QA group's job."

Today, quality best practices have evolved.

Industry best practices have evolved and now place more responsibility for quality with the developers. Today, they are expected to take quality considerations into account as early as the design phase of their work. Unit tests are an integral part of the development tasks for which an engineer is responsible. If a developer follows these best practices, the quality of a product can be quite high. The QA organization can focus its testing efforts on other aspects of product quality like robustness and load testing.

For commercial products, the quality effort is opaque.

There is only one problem with this scenario from the point of view of the user of commercial software. There is no way to know what level of testing has been performed on a product, nor what level of quality the tests themselves reflect. Again, the opaque nature of the commercial software development process makes it difficult to determine how good (or bad) the quality effort has been for any particular product.

Open source makes the quality effort transparent.

Because users have access to the code base of an open source product, they also have access to the QA tests that have been used on the product. The test cases are included as part of the source base and can be examined and run as part of an evaluation process. This enables a very good assessment of how thoroughly the product has been tested during development.

The availability of a product's tests can be used to assess the QA effort for the product and thereby also assess the quality of the product itself. If the QA effort for a product is impressive, it is probable that the product itself is high quality. Therefore, evaluating the QA effort for a product can be a good way to assess the product in question.

Evaluating the QA effort for an open source product helps assess the product's maturity.

Count the Number of Tests

A crude assessment of the quality effort of a product is to count the number of tests that make up the test suite for the product. A good rule of thumb is that every "thing" in a product should be tested. For "thing" substitute the appropriate name for the base level of granularity for the language of the product: class for Java, module for Perl, and so on.

The number of tests should correspond to the number of "things" in a product.

If the number of tests seems small, it might indicate that the quality effort for the product has not been very thorough. A large number of tests indicates that the development team takes the quality process seriously and has devoted significant time to it.

The number of tests is critical.

The number of tests is an easy, quick way to make a rough judgment of the quality effort for the product. If the developers did not devote time to developing tests for the product, it is unlikely that the quality level of the product will be satisfactory.

The number of tests offers a quick assessment of the product's quality effort.

Assess the Tests Themselves

The tests themselves can be reviewed to assess how well they're written. Of course, the tests might not be written in a language: They might be a graphical user interface (GUI) exerciser, or simulate remote procedure calls (RPCs), or any number of testing mechanisms. The point is to look at how the tests are written and

Examine the tests themselves.

assess how good they are. Do they indicate that they are well thought out? Do they seem comprehensive? Is it clear what they are testing?

The quality of the tests is a strong indicator of product quality.

The answers to these questions tell a lot about the quality of the quality process and are a secondary indicator of the quality of the product itself. If the tests seem sloppy or it is not clear what the tests do, it is an indicator that the quality level of the product could be low.

Perform a Test Coverage Assessment

Test coverage assessment tells how thoroughly the product has been tested.

Products are available that will run an existing automated test suite and assess how thoroughly the test suite exercises all of the code branches in a product. This test coverage enables an understanding of how much of the product has actually been tested by a test suite. Naturally, there are open source products that perform this function.

The thoroughness of test coverage can be enlightening.

Running a test coverage tool can be an eye-opening exercise. The first step suggested is to count the number of tests that are available. A large number of tests is positively correlated with good quality generally, and a high percentage of code coverage specifically. However, the number of tests does not conclusively tell how thoroughly the product is tested. There have been situations where large portions of a test suite repeatedly exercise the same portions of a product, whereas other portions of a product go completely untouched. A test coverage exercise can be very useful in understanding how thoroughly the product has been tested.

Poor test coverage might imply poor product quality.

If the test coverage assessment shows good coverage, a high level of confidence in the quality process is appropriate. If the test coverage is unsatisfactory, this does not necessarily indicate that the product quality is low, but it is an indicator of uncertainty and a higher level of risk.

Assess the Activity Level of the Product

It's easy to see what the level of activity is on a project. If it is actively being worked on, it indicates that the development team is making product modifications and improvements, which is a positive indicator of product quality. SourceForge makes an extensive array of project statistics available to help in determining the activity level of a product.

Assess the project's activity level.

Number of Outstanding Bugs

SourceForge lists all outstanding bugs along with a number of ways to sort them. It is easy to see how long bugs have been outstanding, severity levels, and so on. The number of outstanding bugs and how long they have been outstanding gives a good idea of how quickly problems are being addressed, and thereby offers a way to assess how much work is going into improving the quality of a product. A low number of bugs and evidence of quickly addressing bugs indicate an active development effort along with a strong attention to quality issues.

Review the number of outstanding bugs.

Number of Code Checkins

SourceForge offers a source code repository browsing capability; this capability enables the check-in activity at any level of a source tree to be examined, along with actual source changes and comments by the developer.

Review the number of code check-ins.

An assessment of the quality level of the engineering efforts is possible by looking at the check-in activity along with the information accompanying the check-ins. A consistent stream of code modifications indicates that the development team is actively working on the product and improving its quality and functionality. If there have been a small number of recent check-ins, the product is not receiving much attention from the developers. Consequently, there is a risk associated with it, because few improvements are being made to the product.

A high number of code check-ins indicates higher product quality.

Responsiveness to bugs is an indicator of product quality.

By looking at the number of bugs, how quickly they are addressed, and how much activity is going on in the source base, the assessment effort can determine how much attention is paid to quality issues by product team members. Quick attention to bugs reduces the risk of using a product and is a positive indicator of product maturity.

Assessing the Product Team

Product team membership can be easily identified.

Unlike opaque commercial development organizations, open source product developers are easily identified and communicated with. Each project on SourceForge lists the size of the development team and every member's identity and role, including an e-mail link. As used here, the term development team includes all participants in the project, whether their role is engineering, documentation, translation, or QA.

The quality of the product team is a key factor in the maturity of an open source product.

The development team's makeup, experience, and commitment is, perhaps, the key risk factor in an open source product (in fact, it is a key risk for any kind of software, but is usually not directly addressed in commercial software selections). At the end of the day, open source is all about developers cooperating to make products available under an open source license. Depending on how a product is to be used, the availability of an engineer to fix a problem could be critical. Assessing the project team is an important step in assessing product quality.

Examine the Size of the Project Team

Look at team size.

The size of the project team is very instructive. A team that is too small is a risky situation, in that if one member of the team drops out of the product team, problems with the product might not be addressed in a timely manner. There are strategies to mitigate this risk, but it is better if the team is staffed by an adequate number of team members.

The team size is instructive, but not too much should be read into it. Small teams are the norm in development organizations, both commercial and open source, throughout the world. Small teams can be very effective and efficient in their work, so it might not be a problem if the team is small.

Examine the Skills and Experience of the Project Team Members

Because it is simple to communicate with team members, an assessment of the project team is easily performed. Interacting with the product lead, you can gather information about team size and any current issues with team makeup. This interaction also can help assess the skills and experience of the team as well. If the team does not contain individuals with significant experience (remember, the average experience level in open source engineers is 11 years, as indicated by the BCG survey), the risk level of the product can be quite high.

Don't expect the team to be made up only of highly experienced individuals. Every software product has a mix of experience levels in the engineering team and open source is no different. More experienced individuals take on the most significant tasks like architecture and design, whereas less experienced individuals focus on coding, installation, and packaging. In fact, a team with only highly experienced members might be as much of a problem as one with no experienced members, because it might not focus on less challenging, yet important tasks, like easy-to-use product installation.

Don't Be Afraid to Address This Issue

It might seem intrusive to query the project team about its makeup, experience level, and skill distribution. However, assessing the team is so important that it must not be avoided. Naturally, the interaction should be handled tactfully. Most teams are eager to have their product used and are very open about discussing any aspect of the product. If the team is not forthcoming on this issue during the selection process, it is a huge warning flag. One of the biggest fears of using open source is the dependence on a team of volunteers. Almost universally, that fear is unjustified. However, if the interaction indicates a poor level of communication, it is a sign of a higher level of risk. Don't avoid finding out about the development team.

Assigning a Product Maturity Score

Keep a written record during the assessment phase.

During the assessment process of each item, the group doing the assessment should document its findings on the product maturity checklist. A written record of everyone's perception of the quality of each item enables the group to quickly work together to assign the item's final score.

Assign scores individually before discussion.

I recommend that each participant assign a score before any group discussion of the item. This ensures an honest rating unaffected by group dynamics. After each person has assigned his or her score, a list of the scores should be put together and distributed.

Reach a consensus on product maturity.

Once all of the scores have been distributed, a discussion about the group's rating of the element can take place. The goal is to reach a consensus rating that reflects an agreement among all the group's members. The discussion about how the product fared on each item is valuable because it can uncover unspoken assumptions about what the product should do or how it should work.

To reiterate the items to be rated, refer to Table 5.2.

Assign between 0 and 10 points for the product maturity score.

There are 10 possible points available for the product. To determine the product's score, start with the functionality requirements list developed at the start of the assessment process. Determine how fully the product measures up to the requirements. Move on to the product's longevity and make an assessment of the maturity of the overall life span of the product. After the product's longevity has been addressed, consider overall product quality, using the assessment mechanisms outlined in that section of this chapter. Finally, evaluate the development team itself for size and skills.

Product functionality	How well does the product match the functionality requirements developed as the first step in this process?
Product longevity	How long has the product been available?
Product quality	Does the product reflect good quality and good development processes? Is there sufficient testing with good quality tests?
Product team quality	Is the team large enough with the right skill and experience mixture?

Table 5.2
Product Maturity
Items to Be Rated

Based on these four items, assign an overall maturity score for the software element of the entire product. The score should be between 0 and 10.

Here are a few important points about assigning the maturity score:

- This is a judgment call. Some people are uncomfortable assigning a concrete number to something that seems abstract, like how well this product fulfills the functionality requirements or the quality of the development team. Although this seems like an obvious concern, using this technique actually forces a judgment and crystallizes a potentially amorphous process. Most people who initially feel uncomfortable with a numeric judgment come to feel it is a valuable method of expressing a judgment.
- Judgment calls are better when they take into account all information—in this case, the collective judgment of the task force. The process of assigning a score helps draw out

everyone's opinion and ensures that any differences in perspective are ironed out at this stage, rather than being ignored until too late in the process.

- This is a critically important piece of the entire assessment pie. If a product comes up short at this stage, it might be wise to cut short the assessment effort for this product. Although there are ways to mitigate product shortcomings, a product that is woefully short of the necessary software maturity is probably not a good candidate for improvement. The improvement options available are better used to add marginally necessary functionality—the cherry on top, not the foundation at the bottom, to mix a metaphor. Discarding an obviously flawed product at this stage can avoid wasted effort. A rule of thumb is that a product scoring less than 6 should probably not be taken further into the assessment process.

Assessing JBoss: Product Maturity

As you can see from the checklist in Table 5.3, a JBoss product assessment was performed along the four product aspects discussed in this chapter. As a recap, those product aspects are

- Functionality
- Longevity of the product
- Quality of the product
- Quality of the product team

JBoss supports the relevant product standards.

In terms of product functionality, JBoss fully supports the relevant J2EE application server standard and is, in fact, beginning the process of being certified by Sun. JBoss delivers a full J2EE product set via the inclusion of the Tomcat servlet engine. JBoss suffers in comparison with the commercial providers in that they offer additional products integrated with the J2EE product set. Specifically, one commercial vendor offers a tightly coupled development environment that makes creating J2EE applications much easier than hand-coding them. Although JBoss also offers an integrated development environment (IDE) for its product, the IDE is not as complete or as tightly integrated.

JBoss has been around for more than three years—not quite as long as the other J2EE application server products, but a respectable length of time, given that J2EE itself is a relatively recent standard. Because of the large number of downloads, one might say that JBoss is older than it looks, because the amount of use it has gotten is as great or greater than longer lived commercial products that have fewer total users.

JBoss's longevity is more than three years.

The product's quality is quite high. It has relatively few bugs, given the very large number of downloads. The total number of bugs outstanding is not very high, either, and bugs are addressed pretty quickly. A review of randomly selected source indicates good coding practices, although they are only somewhat better than average.

JBoss has relatively few bugs outstanding.

Finally, in terms of the development team, JBoss has a very large development team—nearly 100 members. In discussions with the development team, it became evident that only about a dozen members of the team are truly active in terms of product development; however, that is a good-sized team for an open source project. The developers average more than five years of engineering experience—not as much as open source developers in general, but definitely reflective of significant experience.

JBoss has a large development team.

Overall, the product assessment for JBoss was assigned 8 points out of a possible total of 10. JBoss did not achieve a higher score due to its lack of a fully integrated IDE and its relatively short longevity. If its IDE continues to mature, its product element score will improve in the future.

JBoss received 8 out of 10 possible points for product maturity.

Table 5.3   OSMM Product Assessment Checklist

OPEN SOURCE MATURITY MODEL	
Product Assessment Checklist	
Product Name: JBoss	
Method	**Notes**
Product Functionality	
Reviewed applicable standards: J2EE standard.	JBoss is committed to certifying on Sun J2EE 1.4 Compatibility Test Suite—will offer complete J2EE standards compliance. Certification to be complete mid- to late 2004.
Compared with commercial vendor's published functionality.	JBoss not as strong in integrated development tools, but meets competition in incorporating other products to offer full J2EE functionality (e.g., Tomcat for servlets).
Reviewed technology analyst "best of breed" functionality definitions.	Analysts refer to J2EE standard to define necessary functionality in application server; as noted, JBoss supports J2EE standard and is committed to certification.
Polled user community.	Not applicable for this assessment.
Product Longevity	
Product version number.	Version 3.2 in release; Version 4.0 in beta.
Life span.	First version released in 1999; first registered on SourceForge in March 2001.
Total number of downloads.	4.4 million; consistently ranks around 40th in SourceForge monthly downloads.
Product Quality	
Source code review.	5 .java files reviewed. All written very cleanly with very comprehensible code. 4 of the 5 were well commented (1 outstandingly so); 1 of the 5 had no comments.
QA assessment: Number of QA tests.	Approximately 1,700 tests. JBoss is performing the J2EE certification test suite as part of their certification effort; that test suite contains approximately 23,000 tests.
QA assessment: Review of QA tests.	5 test cases reviewed. Code is good quality, clean, and comprehensible. 2 of the 5 were commented; 3 were not.

Table 5.3   OSMM Product Assessment Checklist *(cont.)*

Method	Notes
Product Quality *(cont.)*	
QA assessment: Test coverage assessment.	Not performed for this assessment.
Activity level of product: Number of outstanding bugs.	1,772 cumulative bugs; 208 outstanding.
Activity level of product: Number of code check-ins.	Product averages 9 patches per month.
Product Team	
Size of product team.	91 members. Team members are not identified by role, but JBoss has confirmed that several focus on documentation and several others focus on QA, although no breakdown is available.
Skill and experience level of team.	JBoss.org has developer profiles. Average commercial experience is 6–10 years. A number of the developers have a Ph.D.

6

Open Source Technical Support

Executive Summary

Built by volunteers with no formal organizational structure, open source products are freely and anonymously available at the touch of a button. Because of this unique structure, services that we take for granted as part of a commercial software offering do not accompany the software. The first question raised about using open source software is always, "Who will take a call?," meaning, "Who will provide support services for this product?" IT managers are naturally reluctant to use a product that appears to have no one standing behind it.

Software in general is difficult to use and often displays buggy behavior, so technical support is a prerequisite for success with any software product. How users receive technical support for open source products is an issue that must be addressed before pragmatic organizations will begin using them.

This chapter presents three options for open source technical support and discusses how they reflect on the maturity of an open source product. The use of commercial support for an open source product is discussed with both the positives and negatives of the approach presented. The technical support maturity scoring is presented, along with a maturity score for the example product, JBoss. A checklist to document information about a product's support options is provided at the end of the chapter.

The Two Types of Technical Support

The term *technical support* actually encompasses two different types of service, which differ significantly in both what they deliver and how critical they are. The first type answers product usage questions: "How do I do this with the product?" The second type solves product failures: "The product isn't working. How can I get it back up and running properly—fast?" When people ask, "Who will take a call?" they are really asking about product failure support. Although product failure support is critical, product usage support is also very important—it can shorten the learning curve for a product significantly and help users quickly address non-emergency problems that might otherwise take days to solve. An organization that is assessing an open source product should consider both types of support in determining the technical support maturity level.

Of the two types of technical support, product failure represents a minority of support requests. About 40 percent of all support requests begin with an assertion that the product is not working, but a large percentage of these requests (on the order of 75 percent) quickly resolve into product usage discussions, meaning that the product is working correctly, but the user isn't aware of the right way to use it. Consequently, of all technical support requests, only about 10 percent represent product failures. Even within these requests, however, there are different types of failures, ranging from minor inconveniences to catastrophic failures. The latter type represents a very small proportion of technical support requests—perhaps half of 1 percent. However, the infrequency of catastrophic failures does not diminish how critical they are. If an organization is depending on a product and experiences a catastrophic failure, it needs an immediate way to address it.

These critical failures are what pragmatic IT organizations are most worried about when they ask how open source technical support is delivered. They don't want to be stranded without someone taking responsibility for fixing their problem, summed up in the piquant phrase, "one throat to choke." This is indeed a critical issue relating to open source technical support. Fortunately, there are ways to address it.

Product failure support is what pragmatic IT organizations are most worried about with respect to open source.

Doesn't Source Availability Mean Technical Support Doesn't Matter?

Because the product source code is available, it might seem that an organization can take responsibility for technical support itself. On the surface, this seems attractive. One of the most frustrating aspects of commercial software is contacting a company for technical support. If the call relates to product usage, all too often the person on the other end of the phone knows less about the product than the caller. This common experience is frustrating, to say the least.

Does open source mean support doesn't matter?

If the call relates to a product failure, many times the response goes something like this: "We know about that problem; it will be fixed in the next release." This is also pretty frustrating. Even if the call relates to a serious product problem, it could take a significant amount of time for the problem to work its way through the company hierarchy until someone addresses it.

Support for commercial software products can be problematic.

However, with source availability, all those problems go away! Problems can be fixed immediately by an organization with minimal downtime. Just make your own change to the product source. Self-sufficiency rules!

Source availability can shortcut support problems.

Unfortunately, it's a bit more complicated than that. Source availability does make it possible for an organization to quickly address problems and solve them in a way that satisfies its needs. Overall,

However, self-support imposes extra costs on organizations.

source availability can help keep systems up and running. However, taking responsibility for a source base also incurs significant costs in terms of personnel and infrastructure. Taking the source code of an open source product in house is usually not a good idea, unless it is part of an overall strategy. A more sophisticated approach that takes advantage of source availability and the strengths of the open source product community is a better way to proceed.

Defining Technical Support Requirements

There are three types of open source technical support.

There are three technical support options available to open source users: community, paid, and self-support. Determining which is the best choice is important for an organization as it selects an open source product. Each option has strengths and weaknesses that should be reviewed; matching the options to the organization's capabilities and intent is important as well. An organization that has very deep technical skills might be more ready to rely on self-support than another with fewer technically talented personnel.

To determine the organization's requirements, it needs to do a self-assessment of its staffing and experience levels. The following sections present some general guidelines for this process.

Assess How Familiar the Organization Is with the Product or a Product Like It

Determine how familiar the organization is with the product.

If the organization is new to the product, it will require more mature support mechanisms, potentially including telephone support for immediate response. If the organization has experience with a similar product, the need for intense support will probably be lower. For example, if it is considering implementing JBoss and already uses another J2EE application server, its needs for intense support will probably be lower. On the other hand, if it is moving to JBoss from a Microsoft-based infrastructure, there will be a steep learning curve, which implies significant support requirements.

Assess How the Product Will Be Used

A product that is used for production purposes requires that support be available very quickly, whereas one used in an internal intranet might allow for slower support response times. Keep in mind that there could be a range of uses and that range might change through the life cycle of the project. For example, developers can usually live with more leisurely support responses, but operations personnel might have more immediate needs. The type of support required might change over time as the product moves from pilot into production use.

The type of use might dictate the type of support required.

Assess the Skill Levels and Attitude of the Individuals Using the Product

Skill levels within groups vary enormously; therefore, depending on who will be responsible for activities requiring support, a higher or lower level of support might be necessary. Responsibilities shift around within IT organizations, so even if the current individuals are highly skilled, someone with a lower level of skill might be assigned at a later date. It is therefore probably a good idea to assess whether the available support mechanisms are satisfactory for the latter type of individual.

The available skill levels might also dictate the type of support required.

The attitude of the individuals who will use support can make a big difference in how successful they will be in using a given support mechanism. The importance of interacting respectfully with community members was discussed in Chapter 5, "The Open Source Product"; however, someone with an active approach can often get help from a support mechanism that another person with a more passive attitude will be unsuccessful with. This is discussed further in "Community Support" on page 129 of this chapter.

The attitude of an organization's personnel can affect how successful its support requests will be.

Documenting Requirements

Based on the self-assessment the organization performs, support requirements should be documented for comparison with the

Identify support requirements.

resources identified in the next step of the process. Documenting the results of the self-assessment enables the organization to explicitly examine its assumptions and practices, avoiding potential problems if the support the organization needs is not available.

The available support options for a product have strong implications for its maturity.

However, beyond selecting the right support option based on the organization's staffing and skill levels, the type of technical support that is available for a particular open source product says a lot about the maturity of the product. The maturity implications of each of the support options are discussed later in the chapter.

Locating Resources

As noted earlier, there are three options for open source technical support:

- Community support
- Paid support
- Self-support

The multiple support options of open source can be a benefit.

It is more difficult to locate open source support resources than it is to do so for commercial products, but there are a number of techniques that can assist the organization in its search. Although the numerous support mechanisms might seem like overkill in comparison with the single-source approach of commercial software vendors, the availability of multiple mechanisms can actually be a strength of open source. Relying on a single provider exposes an IT organization to significant risk.

Community support is an important aspect of open source technical support.

Because community technical support is atypical in the commercial software arena, it is discussed at some length here. Community support can be extremely useful and offers some real advantages including availability, risk reduction, cost, and the ability to leverage other people's expertise.

Community Support

Every open source product has at least one mailing list to allow product users to interact with one another. Some products that are especially popular can have upward of 100 user mailing lists, each devoted to a particular aspect of the product.

Open source products all have mailing lists.

Most mailing lists offer statistics about the list: number of members, number of posts, and so on. There is typically a choice about whether to receive each posting as it is sent or to receive a single e-mail containing a concatenation of all the day's posts. A searchable archive of past postings, organized by month, will also be available. This archive allows you to see if a question has been addressed in the past and shortens the time required to get an answer.

Statistics about product mailing lists are available.

These mailing lists demonstrate one of the real benefits of open source: the community of users. It's easy to reach out and take advantage of others' experience with a product to help solve problems.

Mailing lists make it easy to take advantage of other users' experience.

Mailing List Protocol

There is a protocol to using mailing lists. A posting should ask a question in a succinct way with sufficient information to fully describe the problem. For example, if the product being used is a programming language, a code sample, along with a description of the problem being observed, is expected. If the product being used is an application, a description of the input as well as the error condition is appropriate. Vague or ambiguous questions are often disregarded or criticized. However, mailing lists can be an outstanding method of obtaining support.

Questions to mailing lists should follow the unwritten rules.

Of course, the advice proffered must be assessed as to usefulness. Very often, multiple replies will be posted, each offering different ways to address the problem. Sometimes, the solutions even conflict with one another.

The replies must be assessed, of course.

The Best Use of Mailing Lists

Mailing lists excel
for usage support.

Mailing lists are extremely useful for usage type support, where the support required revolves around how to accomplish something with a given product. Lists lend themselves very effectively to a question–answer interaction, where a problem following the protocol just outlined is posted.

Mailing lists are perfect for the following scenario:

Some aspect of a product seems like it should work, but it just doesn't. Attempt after attempt is made to figure out what to do and all are unsuccessful. After working on the problem for an extended period of time, it seems like the solution is impossible to find. No other potential solutions spring to mind and no experienced coworker is easily available. No documentation at hand addresses the question. What can be done to find the right answer? What you really need is a nudge in the right direction either via a hint or a sample of how to solve the problem.

A posting is placed into the appropriate mailing list. Most lists have very experienced product users who monitor them. They usually know how to solve the problem, or even more likely have suffered through the same problem. They post a response to the problem, offering a way to move forward. The solution is applied to the problem, and what seemed intractable is solved.

This scenario might seem too rosy, but it is a very common experience. Responses to postings often arrive within minutes of the original posting. Solutions come from people literally all over the world.

Mailing List Benefits

Mailing lists can
make it easier to
do one's job.

The scenario just outlined highlights one of the biggest benefits of mailing lists: making it easier to do one's job. Drawing on the experience of others helps solve problems more quickly and reduces frustration. Very often someone else will have dealt with the problem and be able to respond very rapidly with a working solution. This enables you to move forward on the main task at hand, solving a business problem through the application of IT.

Mailing lists are also an excellent way to learn improved methods of working with a product through exposure to the best practices of an entire user community. Very often, more than one solution to a question will be posted; the questioner can compare the solutions and assess the best one, or combine the suggestions to create a better one.

Mailing lists provide exposure to product best practices.

Mailing lists also can serve as a learning resource when you are using a product that does not have mature training or documentation available. An open source product usually develops a significant user community before commercial entities that deliver training or publish books become aware of the product. Consequently, there can be significant use of a product before professional resources are available. In that situation, an organization that begins using a product will not have commercial resources available, making the knowledge base of the user community particularly valuable.

Mailing lists can serve as a training mechanism.

From the perspective of running an IT organization, the rapid responses available from mailing lists can significantly improve the ability of the organization to work efficiently. Harvesting the knowledge of a large user base raises the productivity of an organization's personnel. Knowledge harvesting can also help address production problems as well, reducing system downtime and performance issues, and thereby increasing organizational productivity.

Mailing lists offer rapid responses and increased organizational efficiency.

Mailing List Concerns

Do mailing lists mean "no one is there?"

Relying on the user community for advice in using a product raises an alarm bell for IT managers. It seems that no one is "there," responsible to answer questions. Issues of responsiveness (How soon will the question be answered?) and quality (How much does the person answering the question really know?) are natural areas for concern. The image of open source that many IT managers have causes them to believe that no good support mechanism can possibly be available on an unpaid basis.

A product's mailing list should be assessed before being rejected as a sufficient support mechanism.

The absence of a support organization that is contractually committed to provide support might, indeed, present a risk exposure. Reliable, high-quality, technical support is a must, and the heavy weighting that technical support receives in the OSMM reflects its importance. However, the available user community support might offer sufficiently mature technical support. Certainly, the quality of a product's mailing list should be assessed before concluding that it is an inadequate support mechanism.

How to Use Mailing Lists

Should only specific individuals contact mailing lists?

Mailing list support differs significantly from typical commercial support models. Commercial support usually imposes a requirement that only specified individuals contact technical support with questions. IT organizations then have to implement a process to forward support questions to the identified contacts, who will then contact the vendor on behalf of the question originator. Because this is a familiar model, IT organizations sometimes question whether it should be applied to mailing lists as well.

It is appropriate for multiple members of the organization to post to mailing lists.

In the commercial support scenario, the vendor representative responding to the question acts as a checkpoint, ensuring that only the right people are making support requests. Because mailing lists are easily available to anyone, there is no control imposed on who can post questions. Given the lack of a governing mechanism, it is probably not worth the effort to impose a requirement that only specified individuals post questions to the mailing list. Furthermore, because posting questions and receiving responses offer the opportunity for learning, it is probably not in the organization's interest to even attempt this type of restriction.

Posting Protocol

Some of the best practices for posting to mailing lists were discussed earlier in this section. Questions should be direct and specific, with sufficient example information to enable potential responders to understand the issue at hand. The tone should be respectful to raise the probability of a good quality response.

Be sure postings are complete and specific.

Something that might not be quite so obvious is the need to ensure confidentiality in the posting. It might be necessary to document data values or variable names as part of a posting. These items should be scrubbed to ensure that no confidential organizational or customer data is shared with the mailing list. Any confidential data should be replaced with placeholder information; for example, a real customer name should be replaced with a fictional customer name. Most posters understand this instinctively, but it is worthwhile to document this requirement as part of the process of using mailing list support.

Be sure the posting does not contain proprietary data.

Mailing List Summary

Although the use of mailing lists for technical support is usually a concern to IT managers, mailing lists can provide a valuable resource for open source users. Organizations must determine the best way to take advantage of mailing list support. One question is whether to control the number of people in the organization who can post to the list. Although limiting the number of individuals who can access support resources is common for commercial products, it is probably not a good idea to impose this restriction for mailing lists.

Mailing lists can be a valuable support mechanism.

Whatever the organization decides with respect to who can post, the requirements for posting content are the same:

- Direct, specific questions
- Respectful tone
- No confidential data in posting

MAILING LIST TECHNICAL SUPPORT: CHARLES K. CLARKSON

One question always raised about mailing list technical support is "Who does it and why?"

Charles K. Clarkson is a stalwart of the Perl Beginners Mailing List (PBML), answering 5 to 10 questions each day. His answers are thorough and accurate (my firm has been the beneficiary of his help on a number of occasions). Clarkson offers technical support on the PBML as a way of unwinding from his regular work: real estate investment. When queried about why he participated in offering support on the PBML, he responded:

"I learned about computers during my career at Home Depot, where I worked in a variety of roles. I taught a lot of classes there, and discovered that teaching a subject is the best way to learn it. After 12 years, I left Home Depot to begin investing in Texas real estate.

My work with Perl began as an outgrowth of my real estate work. A local real estate organization had a Perl-based Web site with a Y2K problem. I was able to fix it, but felt I needed a more thorough knowledge of the language. To better learn Perl, I began to lurk the PBML, noting the answers that others gave to the posted questions and seeing how my solutions matched up. Eventually I began to respond to questions myself."

When asked why someone who works in real estate would devote spare time to answering Perl questions, he replied, "All day long I deal with people who behave irrationally when confronted with problems. It's real relaxation to solve programming problems—they're completely logical."

Clarkson's story illustrates something unique about the community support open source offers. It takes advantage of contributions from people who wouldn't be available in a commercial software environment, thereby increasing the pool of knowledge available to draw on.

Paid Support

Paid support is available for some open source products. This type of support is similar to what most people are familiar with from the commercial software world. E-mail is the preferred support mechanism, with more personal support mechanisms available at a higher cost. An organization would typically be expected to identify one or several individuals who would have responsibility for contact with the support organization; other members of the supported organization would be expected to funnel their queries through the responsible individuals.

Paid support is also available for some open source products.

Who Offers Paid Support?

As described in Chapter 2, "Open Source Business Models," open source does not necessarily mean noncommercial. There are for-profit companies that offer open source products, either by commercially distributing a community-based product, or by being the sole distributor of the source code of the product itself. In the latter case, they control the development process and limit the power of individuals to make modifications to the official source base.

Paid support providers can be distributors or the copyright holders of an open source product.

In addition to the open source product itself, these companies offer additional services, the most common of which is technical support. Support services allow customers to directly access dedicated support personnel who will help with usage questions and take responsibility for bug reports. The companies employ engineers who are capable of fixing these bugs and delivering a patched product to the customer.

These organizations offer paid support.

How Much Does Paid Support Cost?

By the standards of commercial software, paid support costs are relatively modest. Commercial support is usually part of a maintenance offering, which gives access to new versions of the product as well as technical support. In effect, support is bundled with

Support for commercial software products can be quite expensive.

discounted access to future versions of the product. Maintenance costs are typically figured as a percentage of the software license fee, usually around 15 to 20 percent. As software licenses can be very expensive, it follows that the maintenance costs themselves can be quite expensive as well.

Open source support costs are typically much less expensive than their commercial counterpart.

Because there is no open source license fee (typically) to which support costs are tied and no reason to pay for future versions of an open source product, open source support costs tend to be very reasonable. The cost of support is usually tied directly to the actual costs of the personnel delivering it. Consequently, you can expect to pay for support at the same rates as general professional services—anywhere from $100 to $400 per hour.

Who Uses Paid Support?

Risk-averse organizations and those uncomfortable with community support are the main users of paid support.

Paid technical support appeals to two types of organizations: those that must be very risk-averse and those that are uncomfortable with community-based support. Organizations that face significant costs from application downtime seek arrangements that give them the greatest confidence that product issues will be addressed immediately. For these organizations, having a dedicated support organization available to respond to problems is worth paying for, even for a product that is available for free. These organizations require that an open source product score very high on the OSMM for all elements, as their risk aversion is very high.

Organizations unfamiliar with open source might also prefer paid support.

Other organizations might not have the same issues as organizations that face significant downtime risks, but will feel more comfortable with a support contract in hand. They might not have much experience with open source products and are unfamiliar with community-based support. Consequently, they will be more confident with a traditional support arrangement in place.

Interestingly, organizations that contract for paid technical support often do not take advantage of it. One open source support provider estimates that its customers utilize no more than 10 percent of the support that is purchased. This statistic illustrates that organizations purchase support as an insurance policy that protects them in case of a catastrophe, rather than a mechanism to help them use the product.

Organizations often do not use the paid support they purchase.

Self-Support

If your organization already uses the product, you might be able to support yourself. For example, if another part of your organization has significant experience with the product, you might be able to leverage that expertise to support a group just beginning with the product. Alternatively, you might hire one or more individuals with expertise in the product to provide support to the rest of the organization as part of their overall duties.

If your organization has significant experience with the product, self-support might be an option.

This support option can be excellent. Usage questions can be answered almost immediately. Product problems can be escalated and worked on very quickly. The individuals providing the support know a lot about your business and therefore can react to problems with great insight. Self-support is probably cheaper than commercial support as well.

Self-support can be significantly less expensive than paid support.

Assessing Technical Support Maturity

Assessing Community Support

The key question about community support is how to determine how good it is. However, how do you do an assessment of the mailing list's maturity before committing to a product and generating actual support requests? There are several factors to examine in making a maturity assessment of community support.

Several factors determine the quality of community technical support.

Number of Mailing Lists

The number of mailing lists is an indicator of community support maturity.

Depending on the product, the number of lists that address product questions can range from one to well over 100. Generally speaking, a new mailing list is created when the traffic on an existing list gets too great, and the product is complex enough to warrant a list devoted to a particular product aspect. The new mailing list must generate enough traffic to make its existence worthwhile.

Be sure that a relevant mailing list is available to you.

If there are several mailing lists available, it indicates a large user community that will provide product support. In addition to the number of mailing lists, the subjects they cover should be assessed to determine if one germane to the organization's particular interests is available. The existence of multiple mailing lists is irrelevant if there is not one that will address the likely questions the organization will generate.

Use the functionality list from the product assessment phase to determine that there is an appropriate mailing list available.

The functionality list created as part of the product assessment phase lists the product areas most important to the organization. The available mailing lists should be examined to confirm that one or more are devoted to the areas deemed most important. If no mailing list support covers an area of importance, there is a significant risk to the organization that should be taken into account when rating the maturity of this element.

Number of Mailing List Members

Look at the number of mailing list members.

Mailing lists usually provide the number of current subscribers. The key to getting good responses to posted questions is how many people read them. A large readership indicates a good-sized user community and implies that there will be high-quality responses. Conversely, if the mailing list has few members, that is a sign that the product is seldom used. Check how many people subscribe to the germane mailing lists.

Traffic on the Mailing List

Once the number of mailing lists has been confirmed, the next step is to assess how much traffic they generate. An important factor in receiving user community support is how active the community is on a particular mailing list. Mailing list archives typically offer a summary of how many postings have been made in a particular time period (usually monthly), so you can easily determine how active the mailing list is. Furthermore, the trend of how many postings are made each month can be examined to see if participation in the mailing list is growing. Growing participation indicates a growing user community, which reduces support risk and indicates growing product maturity.

Look at how much traffic there is on the mailing list.

A list that has little traffic indicates that few people are concerned about the product. This is an indicator of significant risk because a small user community for a product is a warning signal that the product is quite immature.

Low traffic indicates a small user community.

Quality of Postings

Another indicator of the quality of a mailing list is the postings themselves. To assess the quality of postings, select a few at random and review them. Clearly stated problems are a good sign of the quality of the user base. The responses, are, of course, critical. Are the responses on subject? Do they directly address the question raised? Do they offer specific advice or solutions? Review the postings to see how good the technical advice is, because it indicates the quality of the product's user community.

Review the quality of the mailing list postings.

Another element of postings just as important as the technical information they contain is their tone. If the responses are condescending or arrogant, that is a warning sign. No matter how good the information in a posting is, if it makes the original questioner feel stupid, the mailing list will not be a good support resource.

Review the tone of the postings as well.

If the tone is poor, that can signal trouble if you depend on community support.

The natural tendency to avoid this "you are stupid for asking this question" situation has important implications for your organization. If people do not take advantage of the user community, problems will not be solved as rapidly and will hinder your organization's progress. Therefore, examining the tone of the responses is just as important as assessing their content. This type of problem does not occur very often, but mailing list postings should be examined to ensure it does not exist.

Responsiveness of Postings

Examine how responsive the replies to postings are.

Another factor to assess about mailing lists is how responsive they are to postings. What you are trying to determine is how quickly a posting by a member of your organization is likely to receive a response. In general, the more quickly postings are responded to, the better—assuming, of course, that the responses are of high quality.

There are two easy tests to determine responsiveness.

There are two ways to assess the list responsiveness. The first is to examine a number of questions to see how quickly they have received responses. The second is to do an experiment. Post a question—the best type is one that is similar to what your organization would be posting generally—and see how quickly the question receives responses. This is an acid test. If the responses arrive quickly, you can be confident in the quality of the mailing list. However, if the responses trickle in slowly and are not very useful, the quality of the mailing list is low, which should be reflected in the OSMM score.

The responsiveness of many mailing lists is excellent.

Our experience is that the response time of mailing lists is generally excellent. On a number of occasions, postings have been responded to in less than half an hour with excellent solutions, with responses from all over the world. This has made our projects run very efficiently. We have seen some mailing lists that have low usage or poor quality responses, which has motivated us to find substitute product solutions.

Maturity Implications of Mailing List Support

The quality of a product's mailing list support is a very strong indicator of the maturity level of a product. Products with small mailing list membership or few postings to the mailing list are not widely used and therefore are low in maturity. Naturally, the quality of the postings also has implications for the product's maturity. If the postings are direct and businesslike, the user community is likely using the product in a production role, which of course indicates a higher maturity level.

> The maturity of community support can be determined by the quality of the mailing lists.

If a product has multiple mailing lists, there is a large user community. This is strongly correlated with a higher product maturity level. Essentially, multiple mailing lists spring up to focus on specific product aspects and to avoid overwhelming any particular mailing list with postings. The level of traffic across all the mailing lists reflects the overall user community size, which goes hand in hand with the product's maturity.

> A large number of mailing lists is a strong indicator of product maturity.

Assessing Paid Support

If you are considering purchasing support, how can you assess it during your selection process? Clearly, if you are considering purchasing support as an insurance mechanism, you want to know how others feel the support has worked for them in emergency situations. Even if your interest is not limited to emergency support, you'll want to understand how well it works for routine questions. Several mechanisms exist for you to use to assess the quality and responsiveness of paid technical support.

> How can you assess the maturity of paid support?

Use Paid Support During the Assessment Process

If you can purchase support for a pilot implementation that might be part of your assessment process, do so. Be sure to make several queries during the pilot to see how well the support organization

> Assess paid support during a pilot implementation.

responds. To assess its ability to respond to emergency outages, create one. Deliberately cause a serious problem and see how quickly you are able to get the system back up with the assistance of the support organization.

Check References

Check references from support users.

Ask the support provider for several references. Be sure that they are high-quality references; that is, organizations with similar applications and requirements to yours. Don't be put off or accept poor-quality references. Dig into this and insist you get what you need. You're betting on the ability of the group to support your application; make sure you speak to someone who can give you good feedback on the abilities of the support provider.

Assess the Contract

Determine if the contract fits your support needs.

After you have assessed the quality of the support provided, be sure to look over the details of the support contract. Does it cover all installations of the product throughout your organization, or will you need to make additional payments if you implement more copies of the product? Are you limited in the number of support requests you can make? Above all, find out what modes of contact are available. If the only way to contact the support organization is via e-mail, you might not be much better off than if you just used the product mailing lists.

Assessing Self-Support

Self-support must be assessed as well.

Even if you will use internal resources for self-support, it is important to assess how effective this mode of support will be in practice. There are two primary risk exposures in using self-support: The depth of product knowledge might not actually be that deep in your experts, and, even if product knowledge is deep, you could be exposed to risk because you're dependent on just one or two people. What happens if they leave the company?

During your assessment it should become clear whether your product experts really know the product. Pose several questions to see how well they answer. The quality of response should tell you a lot about the depth of expertise.

Do your in-house experts really know the product?

With respect to the risk exposure of relying on just one or two individuals, it's important to be aware of the situation and be ready to respond if it occurs. Even if you have expertise on staff, be sure to assess the other support options like mailing lists and paid support. That way, even if you do suffer a personnel loss, you will know what your other options are and can readily to move to one of them.

Be aware of risk exposure due to shortness of staff.

Finally, even if the depth and risk issues are addressed to your satisfaction, make sure that the individuals who will provide support have sufficient resources to address the questions that the organization will generate. Self-support is only a good option if the necessary resources are truly available.

Also be sure that the individuals providing support have adequate resources available.

Assigning a Technical Support Maturity Score

For most organizations and most products, the community will be the primary means of technical support, which is why so much emphasis has been placed on it in this chapter. Consequently, community support should account for approximately 60 percent (or 6 points) of the overall maturity score for technical support. Table 6.1 shows the potential points that can be assigned to each support option.

Community support is a critical determinant of product support maturity.

Commercial support can be a valuable support mechanism; just as important, however, is the maturity implication of commercial support availability. Even if you have no intention of using a commercial support provider, the fact that commercial support is available is a strong sign of product maturity, because commercial support

Commercial support can also indicate product maturity.

organizations come into existence only when a product is very well established. Therefore, if commercial support is available, up to three additional points can be assigned to the support maturity score.

Self-support does not necessarily imply overall product support maturity.

Finally, if you have expertise already employed in your organization (or plan to hire one or more individuals with expertise), an additional point is possible. You are very fortunate to have this option available; however, having expertise on staff is not correlated with overall support maturity for the product, so it accounts for only a single point.

The point assignments can be adjusted according to organizational requirements.

Naturally, in terms of an assessment your organization performs, the number of points for each option should serve as a guideline. If the requirements you identified at the beginning of this element's assessment indicated that paid, on-call support is critical for your application, more points should be assigned to that option and it should be assessed appropriately.

Table 6.1
OSMM Point Assignments for Support

Type	Points
Community support	6
Paid support	3
Advanced self-support	1
Total support potential points	10

Assessing JBoss: Technical Support

JBoss has a number of support options available.

JBoss offers a number of support forums, which are monitored by users as well as JBoss employees. In addition, JBoss offers paid support, both for development and production. Both the forums and paid support were assessed during this part of the process. For this assessment, the self-support option was not applicable and therefore not rated. The point assignments for JBoss support are listed in

Table 6.2. For details of the JBoss technical support assessment process, please see Table 6.3. Notes about the assessment are documented on the checklist.

There are a number of support forums available on the JBoss.org site. As you can see from the checklist in Table 6.3, the tone of the postings is very respectful. However, a number of postings receive no responses, which detracts from the quality of support offered. A support mechanism that is hit-and-miss is imperfect, at best. Therefore, only four of a possible six points were assigned for this item.

> Though a number of JBoss support forums are available, many postings on those forums go unanswered.

Several commercial support users were queried about their experience. The overall feedback was quite positive regarding the responsiveness and quality of support. The only drawback is that JBoss offers support only via e-mail and phone; no on-site support is available. (Note: JBoss has recently made on-site support available, but it is a nascent service. The true availability of on-site support should be assessed as part of the paid support assessment.) For some situations, particularly in critical outages, an on-site presence could be necessary. Because of the confusion about on-site availability, only two of the possible three points were assigned for the paid support portion of the assessment.

> JBoss's paid support is praised by users.

Overall, JBoss received 8 of a possible 10 points. If an assessing organization wanted to raise these totals, it could hire one or more experienced JBoss users who could act as internal resources for the rest of the organization.

> JBoss was assigned 8 out of 10 possible points.

Type	Points
Community support	6
Paid support	2
Advanced self-support	0
Total support points	8

Table 6.2
JBoss's OSMM Point Assignments for Support

Table 6.3   OSMM Support Assessment Checklist

OPEN SOURCE MATURITY MODEL	
Support Assessment Checklist	
Product Name: JBoss	
Method	**Notes**
Support Assessment	
Reviewed mailing lists.	There are 14 mailing lists (forums) at the JBoss.org site. Tone of postings is very straightforward and respectful. Some postings receive a number of replies, but a significant number receive no replies. Unclear what posters do to address the problems they have posted about.
Assessed paid support.	JBoss offers two levels of support: developer and production. Support is offered on a prepaid, per-hour basis. General feedback from support clients is positive, no complaints, although it is noted that all support is done via phone; no capability to provide on-site support, even if desired.
Assessed self-support.	Not applicable for this assessment; however, many organizations have significant J2EE expertise on staff who can act as support mechanism.

7

Open Source Documentation

Executive Summary

Documentation is a critical resource when working with software. Software's complexity demands that accurate and helpful documentation be available. Lack of good documentation for an open source product can stop a project in its tracks as team members pore through incomplete or unhelpful documentation.

Beyond its importance as a resource for open source success, the state of a product's documentation implies a great deal about the maturity of an open source product. Product documentation goes through predictable stages as the product matures. Assessing what stage a product's documentation is at offers insight into how mature the product is.

The three types of product documentation are reference, tutorial, and usage (usage is more advanced material of the "tips and tricks" variety). Each of them can be created by the development team or the user community. For some open source products, commercially published documentation of all three types might be available as well. This chapter describes the three types of documentation and how they will affect your use of an open source product. The chapter closes with a discussion of the maturity implications of documentation, along with an assessment of how our example OSMM product, JBoss, stacks up.

Defining Documentation Requirements

The need for documentation differs for each organization depending on its experience level.

The type of documentation an organization will require depends on the use it will make of the product as well as the experience level of its personnel. If an organization is just getting started with a product, tutorial and reference documentation is vital, but advanced usage material is probably not as germane. On the other hand, if advanced functionality of the product is going to be used, or if it will be used at high levels of performance, it will be important to have more advanced material available, offering help for more challenging topics.

Likewise, if the organization's personnel are already familiar with a similar product or are perhaps very experienced in general, tutorial documentation might not be so important, whereas thorough reference material that provides quick information on specific questions will be.

Locating Resources

The source of product documentation changes as the product matures.

There are three sources of open source documentation: the development team, the user community, and commercial publishers. Each has strengths and weaknesses, and each occurs at different stages of an open source product's life cycle. Each source can deliver high-quality documentation, but, unlike commercial software documentation, there is much more variability in the quality levels of open source documentation.

Developer-Created Documentation

The development team delivers reference documentation early in a product's life.

The first source of documentation for an open source product is members of the development team. They deliver basic reference documentation at the time of software release, usually the bare minimum for an experienced developer or administrator to be able to use the product. Remember, reference documentation is not aimed at novice users of the product, but rather at more experienced users. Consequently, this early documentation is most useful for highly technical users and is therefore adequate only for a small user community.

Developer-created reference documentation is usually accurate, but the quality will vary widely depending on the individual developer. With multiple authors and no single individual overseeing the documentation process to ensure consistency and thoroughness, you might find inconsistency in a product's early documentation, depending on which member of the team prepared the portion you examine.

The quality could vary depending on the individual engineer.

Even when each of the engineers is motivated to do a good job, there are several reasons why developer-created documentation can be poor:

- Software engineers look on writing documentation as a less-than-welcome burden and usually put it off until very late in the process. This causes them to give the task less time and attention than it deserves. Hastily created documentation can be inaccurate or confusing, which causes it to be less useful for readers.
- Software engineers are often poor writers. Their skill is writing software, not describing how it works or how to use it. Poor writing skills result in poor documentation.
- Software engineers unwittingly might write poor documentation because they lack "untrained eyes" for the task of writing documentation. They are so familiar with the product that they unconsciously assume a level of knowledge in the reader about the software. The documentation fails to provide enough context and depth for inexperienced users.

This documentation type is best suited for experienced users.

Because developers usually write reference documentation and are not necessarily gifted in documentation skills, this type of documentation is best suited for a highly skilled audience already very familiar with the product.

Web Postings

Web-based postings are a second source of documentation.

As people begin to use an open source product, they encounter problems, learn how to use the product, and, given the spirit of the open source community, want to share their experience with others. They create a second source of documentation: Web-based postings. These postings focus on tutorial and usage rather than reference material.

They are usually short and focused on specific aspects of a product.

These postings take the form of Web pages written by users and placed on their own Web sites. The postings are usually quite short and focused on a particular aspect of the product, although occasionally someone will create a more in-depth tutorial and post it. Web postings can be very useful in solving specific problems. Sometimes code snippets or configuration options will be placed on the page and can be downloaded for use.

You might find this documentation via Web searches.

This type of documentation can be found by doing Web searches—essentially, by poking around on the Web to see what's available. Do not underestimate the usefulness of Web postings because of their seemingly random availability. They can be very useful and their availability reflects the community spirit of the open source world.

The usefulness of Web-based documentation varies.

There are drawbacks to this type of documentation, however. Its randomness and dependence on the effort of community-spirited individuals means that it is a crapshoot whether someone has solved and posted about *your* problem. Generally, there is no attempt by the poster to offer a comprehensive solution or a consistent approach to solving problems. Web postings are analogous to walking down the street and asking your neighbor if he or she has ever seen a particular problem and, if so, how he or she solved it. Depending on your neighbor's knowledge or ability, the answer might be brilliant or useless. Furthermore, the quality of Web postings varies depending on the writing *and* technical ability of the poster. Some postings might be enormously helpful; others could lead you down a dead end, and some might propose something that doesn't work at all.

Web postings occur because someone decided to share his or her experience with a product. Although these postings can be valuable, it's important to keep in mind that they offer extremely spotty documentation. In no sense can they be considered organized and comprehensive. Because the postings occur on Web sites scattered around the Internet, they suffer from a significant lack of community oversight. Unlike documentation that is made available at the project home, which is subject to peer review and suggestions for improvement, Web postings have no community quality control, so the quality of the postings must be assessed individually.

The quality of this documentation can vary as well.

Because of their spotty nature and inconsistent quality, Web-based postings are most useful for experienced users who need "fill-in" documentation, but should not be relied on by new users of an open source product.

This is best suited as "fill-in" documentation.

Commercially Published Documentation

Commercial publishers are a third source of open source documentation; they might offer all three types of documentation for a given open source product. Commercially published documentation offers a number of advantages:

Commercial documentation offers a number of advantages.

- Publishers choose authors of commercially published documentation because of their subject matter expertise. They have significant experience with the product they are writing about and can speak authoritatively about it. This is in contrast to Web postings, in which the writer might or might not have deep experience with the product.

- These authors also must be able to write clearly so that their material is comprehensible. Commercial publishers do not use writers who cannot communicate concepts clearly. This distinguishes commercial documentation from documentation created by the development team, which is often written by someone who specializes in programming, not writing. Even if the author does not possess excellent writing skills, commercial publishers have employees on staff to ensure the resulting documentation is well-written.

- Furthermore, a commercially published book will have been reviewed by a number of technically qualified people during the writing process. This ensures that the material is clearly written and does not suffer from the "untrained eyes" issue described earlier. A commercial book is unlikely to unconsciously assume a level of knowledge inappropriate to a typical reader. This review process ensures that documentation errors and ambiguities are identified and corrected, so that the book is well organized and easy to comprehend.

- Commercial books must comprehensively discuss their subject. Spotty coverage of the topic would doom the book to failure, so publishers insist that the book's topic is thoroughly covered, unlike Web postings that make no attempt at comprehensiveness.

Assessing Documentation Maturity

Each of the documentation types should be assessed for a product.

The recommended strategy is to assess the available documentation for each of the types already described. An ideal situation is to use each type during a pilot program where real-world problems will be encountered and the adequacy of the documentation can be determined. However, it might not be feasible to implement a pilot program for the software product in question. If not, other methods are available to assess the quality of the product's documentation. These methods are appropriate to use whether a pilot is undertaken or not.

Assessing Reference Documentation

If a pilot program is part of the overall assessment exercise, the reference documentation should be used throughout the exercise. The quality of the reference documentation should be assessed during and at the conclusion of the pilot program. If the pilot project highlights gaps in product coverage or ambiguity in the quality of the documentation, those should be documented as part of the final project assessment document.

Reference documentation should be used during a pilot project.

If the pilot project does not fully explore the reference documentation or a pilot project is not feasible, then scenarios that explore the reference documentation should be developed. These scenarios can then be used to determine how well the reference documentation addresses these scenarios. For example, if you are assessing JBoss but cannot implement a pilot project, scenarios would be created that explore how well the JBoss documentation describes how to do a number of tasks. One such scenario might be to determine how well the documentation answers the question, "How can you expose a bean as a Web service?" After all of the scenarios have been run through, an assessment of the quality of the reference documentation for the product can be entered into the documentation checklist.

You might need to create scenarios for using the reference documentation.

Assessing Tutorial Documentation

The key issue for tutorial documentation is how well it prepares a new user to begin using a product. Tutorials do not create experienced users; rather, they create experienced beginners. A tutorial should significantly shorten a new user's learning time frame.

Tutorials should be assessed on how much they shorten the product learning curve.

153

Have someone
unfamiliar with
the product go
through the
tutorial.

Consequently, the best way to assess an open source's tutorials is to assign one or more users unfamiliar with the product to work through the tutorial. Formal criteria for what expectations the organization has for the tutorial should be prepared before someone goes through it. Part of establishing the criteria should be an assessment of the experience level of the majority of people who will eventually take the tutorial. Ideally, the people assigned to work through the tutorial will reflect that typical experience level.

Assess the tutorial
in writing in the
documentation
checklist.

After the people who are trying it have worked through the tutorial, a written assessment of the tutorial quality and appropriateness for the organization can be put into the documentation checklist in preparation for the OSMM assessment.

Assessing Usage Documentation

It might be
difficult to
assess usage
documentation in
a pilot project.

Usage documentation is, by its very nature, focused on specialized and advanced product functionality and experienced users. For that reason, it is often difficult to assess a product's usage documentation in the context of a pilot project, because pilots are usually simple applications that run for limited durations.

Develop scenarios
for product
use and review
the usage
documentation
for those
scenarios.

For these reasons, the best way to assess usage documentation in the absence of an extended product trial is to envision scenarios for potential product use and seek answers for those scenarios in the usage documentation. The scenarios should be constructed to address functionality within the product that the organization is likely to want to use in the future. Each scenario should be used to examine the usage documentation to assess how easily the scenario can be addressed with the information available in the documentation. Again, your findings should be placed in the documentation checklist.

Taking Advantage of the Community's Experience

It is rare that an organization will be the first to use the available documentation for a product. Queries regarding the quality and thoroughness of all three types of documentation can be posted to product mailing lists to get a sense of how satisfied other users and organizations have been with the available documentation.

Query the product mailing lists for assessment of the documentation.

The best way to take advantage of the community's experience is to post specific questions rather than general queries such as, "How good is the documentation for this product?" Questions along the lines of "How well does the product tutorial prepare someone who has the following level of experience for getting up to speed on this product?" will garner more detailed feedback and be a better basis for determining a product's documentation quality.

Post specific questions about the documentation.

Because you prepared scenarios that described areas of the product that your organization is most interested in, it makes sense to focus your postings on these areas. Querying other users about their experience in these areas can offer good insight into the state of the product's documentation. Of course, you will need to emphasize that you're interested in how well the documentation addresses these questions. Otherwise you're likely to find a generous user offering a solution to the problem rather than feedback about how well available documentation addresses it!

Focus your postings on the usage scenarios you developed.

Assigning a Documentation Maturity Score

The type of documentation that is available for a product offers significant insight into the maturity of a product. If the only documentation that is available is that created by the project team, the product is probably fairly new and not widely used. This is typical of

Documentation is a good indicator of product maturity.

an early-stage, immature product. A significant number of Web postings imply that there is a good-sized user base and that the product is at least fairly mature, although the reservations about the quality and thoroughness of user-posted documentation should be kept in mind.

Commercial documentation implies a very mature product.

Commercial documentation that is published by a professional publisher implies a very mature product with a significant current and potential user base. Because commercial publishers only publish books when they believe a sizable market exists for the subject, the availability of commercial documentation can be taken as an indicator of significant product maturity.

You can adjust the point assignments depending on your organization's needs.

Documentation is assigned 10 potential points in the OSMM model. As described already, the three types of documentation (developer-created, user-posted Web postings, and commercial) imply ascending levels of maturity. Table 7.1 presents the default OSMM point assignments for documentation. You might choose to adjust the default point assignments depending on the documentation requirements of your organization.

Table 7.1
OSMM Point
Assignments for
Documentation

Type	Points
Developer-created	2
Web postings	3
Commercially published documentation	5
Total documentation potential points	10

Developer-created documentation reflects a low level of product maturity.

Documentation created by the development team is available very early in a product's life cycle and therefore indicates very little about the maturity of the product. Consequently, only 2 points are assigned for developer-created documentation.

Web postings begin to appear as the product matures and the user community grows. If there are many Web postings, it indicates a healthy user community that is very involved with the product and willing to share its experience. A total of three points are possible if there are Web postings about the product. You can assign an appropriate number between zero and three, depending on the findings outlined in the documentation checklist.

Web-based postings appear as the user community grows and the product matures.

Commercially published documentation appears only when the product is very well established, with a large enough user community to purchase a significant number of copies. A total of five points can be assigned if commercially published documentation is available. The point total can be varied according to your assessment of the quality of the documentation. If a large number of published books are available you might wish to reflect that fact in the score you assign to this item.

Commercially published documentation reflects a high level of product maturity.

With respect to the point assignments for each of the sources of documentation, you should keep in mind that you can adjust the actual assigned points depending on the quality of the documentation in question. Although Web postings can be considered a sign of increased maturity, if all of them are poorly written and inaccurate, it would be appropriate to assign only one or possibly two points to this item. This issue crops up in the JBoss documentation discussion in the next section.

You can adjust the point assignments depending on the quality of the documentation.

Assessing JBoss: Documentation

An OSMM documentation assessment for JBoss is contained in Table 7.2. It reflects an assessment of the available documentation for JBoss and the notes contained in the documentation assessment checklist in Table 7.3 on page 159.

Table 7.2
JBoss OSMM
Documentation
Assessment

Type	Points
Developer-created	2
Web postings	2
Commercially published documentation	2
Total documentation points	6

JBoss made professionally developed documentation available early in the product life cycle.

The JBoss project is a bit unusual in its approach to documentation. In an atypical step for an open source product, a documentation specialist was added to the development team early on and he created fairly comprehensive, well-written reference material. This documentation is available as a free download but is also available in a commercial format that can be purchased. Therefore two points have been assigned for developer-created documentation.

There are many JBoss Web-based postings.

There are a large number of Web postings about JBoss; however, many of them are quite sketchy and difficult to follow. Consequently, only two of a possible three points have been assigned to this item, as it would not necessarily be easy to take advantage of these postings.

There are several JBoss commercially published books, but their quality varies considerably.

There are currently two commercially published books available for JBoss, with another two that will soon be available. User community feedback on the available books is actually pretty negative, although many of the comments note that the documentation available from the developers is quite good. The consensus opinion seems to be that one of the commercially published books is a poor rewrite of the product documentation available from JBoss; the other two would be most useful for experienced JBoss users. As an overall assessment of the commercially published documentation, it would have to be said that its availability indicates a very mature product, but that its poor quality detracts from its usefulness. Therefore, only two points are assigned for the commercially published documentation item.

The overall OSMM documentation point total for JBoss is six. See the documentation checklist in Table 7.3 for more detailed information about the documentation assessment process.

Table 7.3   OSMM Documentation Assessment Checklist

OPEN SOURCE MATURITY MODEL	
Documentation Assessment Checklist	
Product Name: JBoss	
Method	**Notes**
Documentation Assessment	
Reviewed developer-created documentation.	Much more thorough than typical open source developer-created documentation. Available for purchase as well as for free.
	Primarily reference oriented.
	Several favorable feedback items on Amazon postings about commercially published documentation (for additional comments about commercial documentation, see below).
Reviewed Web postings.	Widely available.
	Postings tend to be succinct, even laconic in comparison with postings for other open source products.
	Need to be fairly sophisticated J2EE and JBoss user to take advantage of these postings.
Reviewed commercially published documentation.	Two books currently available, with two due out shortly (no details available about them).
	One book is written by JBoss project lead.
	Reviews of available books on Amazon:
	The book written by JBoss project lead is described as useful to understand product internals, but not as a tutorial or usage guide.
	The other is scathingly described as a rehash of the quite good product documentation available from JBoss.

8

Open Source Training

Executive Summary

Product training is important for any organization using a new product. IT products are complex and difficult to learn. Training employees offers real financial benefits, as demonstrated by one study of training effectiveness. A large survey was conducted of individuals using an enterprise software application. It found that individual productivity rose 20 percent for individuals who attended training, and the time required to master the new application was reduced by 24 percent. The financial implications of the study are quite clear: Training pays off.

There are many training options available for open source products. The user community can be very generous in sharing product information with new users, and product developers might create product tutorials and make them available at the product Web site. Other options also exist for commercial training offerings. In total, there are five options for open source product training:

- Informal Web-based how-to examples posted by product users
- Developer-created online tutorials
- Commercially published tutorials
- Classroom training developed and delivered by the open source development team
- Classroom training developed and delivered by commercial entities

However, the decentralized nature of open source products means that the development team has little control over training materials. Anyone can proclaim that they are a training resource for an open source product. IT organizations seeking training for their personnel must carefully assess the quality of the training providers and their training materials.

This chapter discusses the open source training options available to IT organizations. There are many training options available; the challenge is to locate and assess them. The chapter outlines a number of methods to locate training materials and discusses the maturity implications of the available training for a product. It closes by assessing the training maturity for our example product, JBoss.

Defining Training Requirements

The need for training varies according to the organization's experience level.

Defining the organization's training requirements is very similar to the process used for documentation. The general experience level of the organization's employees helps define how much training is necessary. More experienced employees are usually better at learning material quickly, whereas less experienced employees have less context in which to place new material, making their training needs higher. Also, if you are implementing an open source product that is similar to a commercial product already used in the organization, the employee population already has a good knowledge base and will require less training.

The type of training needed also depends on factors like size of audience and geographical dispersion.

Beyond these obvious observations, there are several items to consider when defining the organization's training requirements. If the product is going to be widely used, it is more important that a consistent, formal training program be put into place. When small numbers of people use a product, they can have rich enough communication to overcome differences in the way they've learned to use the product. When large numbers of people use a product, it is important that they be able to quickly communicate about the product, which is possible if they have a common training background on the product.

If the organization is decentralized, it has the same effect as if large numbers of employees are using the product. Communication in decentralized environments is less rich, and therefore understanding built on common training materials is very helpful.

If the time frame for product implementation is short, formal training methods are appropriate, as they can be used to ensure that everyone is familiar with the product within a given time frame. Less formal training options might deliver the same information, but rely on individuals applying themselves to the material; a short fuse for implementation might not allow for extended learning durations.

Finally, the organization's culture might influence the choice of training options. Many organizations are strong believers in formal training programs. They would require formal tutorials or even classroom training as part of product implementation. Other organizations are less committed to formal training and would be more willing to use Web-based postings or self-paced tutorials.

Based on these factors, the organization should define the training program it would like to use in its open source project. With this set of requirements in hand, it can see how satisfied it is with the product training options that are available for a given product.

Locating Resources

Training options available for open source software products become more formal as the user community grows. Early training alternatives are often informal tutorials, designed for specific product uses, with no effort expended to make the material generally applicable. As an open source product increases its user base and is used by commercial IT organizations, commercial training alternatives spring up, because IT organizations are willing to invest capital in employee training. The traditional life cycle of open source product training moves from user-created, informal, specific materials to professionally developed, generally oriented offerings. Overall, there are five options available for training an organization's employees.

Option 1: Informal Web-Based How-To Examples Posted by Product Users

Early users share their knowledge freely.

Early users of open source products are often evangelists for the product and are very willing to help others make use of the product. Many times they are the experts in a fairly good-sized organization who need to create easy-to-follow instructions for a less technically astute user base. For example, many universities use open source products because of their low cost; as new students enter school, they must be given instructions on how to set up their machines to work with university networks and systems.

They share their experience via the Web.

These early users make their instructions widely available by posting them on Web pages. In the case of a university, new users are expected to follow the instructions as part of their use of the university infrastructure. The training will be a brief introduction to the product along with university-specific installation and configuration instructions.

This training is developed early in a product's life cycle.

Informal Web-based training springs up quite early in an open source product's life. Early users are eager to share how the product has made their work (or life) easier, and, of course, the ease of publishing something to the Web encourages information sharing. This is not to say that this type of training dies out as a product becomes more mature. As the size of a user community grows and other forms of training become available, informal Web-based training continues to grow, with new community members posting new examples.

It's quite easy to find this type of training. A Web search will usually turn up a number of examples that can be easily accessed. Entering the name of the product along with "tutorial" or "training" will provide appropriate links.

The fact that this form of training is so easily created has its downside, however, for pragmatic organizations needing to train personnel. Because anyone can create this form of training, the quality level can be very erratic. Very often the writer makes assumptions about the user's environment or skill level that might be appropriate for the intended audience, but inappropriate for other readers. The examples are often tied to particular implementations or standards that might be inapplicable to other organizations. Simply put, for many of these postings, the writer is creating training materials designed to help someone who has a particular setup solve a particular problem.

This specificity makes it difficult for other organizations to efficiently use this training. New users do not have enough product familiarity to separate general material from specific examples and might find it difficult to draw general lessons about the product from the training material.

From an organizational perspective, it can be difficult to ensure consistency of training with this type of material. Individuals conduct their own searches and make their own selections. They might select material that discusses issues in different or even contradictory ways. Using this type of training makes it impossible to ensure that a consistent quality level is achieved during the training process.

Even when there are no specific environmental assumptions or organizational standards that affect the training materials, there could be other issues present. The training creator might not write clearly or unambiguously. He or she might supply examples that reflect personal preferences, not general methods. Finally, of course, the creator could just be wrong in the training he or she writes. The lack of quality control that might accompany this type of training makes it difficult to uncritically accept it as a basis for training one's own personnel. This type of training is best used when the material can be very specifically applied to a particular environment or when the learner has a good general understanding of the product and is seeking specific information on a particular aspect of it.

Option 2: Developer-Created Online Tutorials

Developers sometimes create online tutorials.

Open source developers sometimes create tutorials to aid new users in familiarizing themselves with the product. These tutorials are online and available at the product Web site. The point in the product life cycle at which these tutorials are created can vary enormously, as their creation depends on the motivation and free time of the training developer.

The material is usually generally applicable.

The creators of a product usually have a very good perspective on the general functionality of the product and avoid writing the training with a bias for a particular environment or a specific way of doing things. In this way, they avoid the problem that is often present in user-written Web-based tutorials—overly focused with little consideration of the range of situations in which the product might be used. Because of this perspective, the tutorial's examples are ordinarily organized to illustrate a general lesson about the product's functionality. Naturally, the fact that a developer writes the tutorial also avoids the problem of the training writer making mistakes about the product.

It might not be easy to use.

The drawbacks to online tutorials created by the developers are less obvious. First, the material is online, which is not always a convenient way to work. Printed material is very easy to flip through to review previously covered material or to quickly find a new topic that the reader wants to learn. The index makes it easy to look at all the places in the book a particular topic is referenced. Of course, it is also extremely handy to have printed training materials sitting next to your computer while you try and work with a product; online materials are very inconvenient in this respect.

A second drawback to developer-created tutorials is the fact that developers are usually not very experienced at developing training materials. The skill set of a training developer is very different than that of a software engineer. Good training has lessons that progressively build on previous lessons to ensure continuity of learning. Of course, the same problem noted in the chapter on documentation is present in developer-created training as well: Engineers often aren't very good writers. This can make the training materials awkward and hard to follow.

The training materials might not be well-designed.

Consequently, developer-created tutorials are a double-edged sword. Developers have a good perspective on the overall usefulness of the product and take pains to demonstrate it. This avoids the issue of material that is too narrowly focused. Developers certainly know the product comprehensively and are unlikely to make mistakes about how it works. On the other hand, the training might not flow well with material designed to present successively more difficult examples. It might not be written very well, either.

Developer-created training might not be well-written.

IT organizations seeking to make use of this type of training should assess whether it is well suited for the learning abilities of the employees who need to be trained. If there is a good match, this can be a very cost-effective method of training and should be seriously considered.

This can be a very cost-effective method of training.

Option 3: Commercially Published Tutorials

Commercial publishers often distribute tutorials.

As described in the previous chapter, commercial publishers often publish books that provide tutorial material. These books usually are oriented to new users of a product and provide an incremental introduction to the product beginning with the very basics.

The tutorials are professionally created.

The benefits to an organization of having commercially published tutorials available are numerous. The material is well-written and carefully reviewed throughout the writing process. This ensures the training is easy to follow and unambiguous.

It's easy to ensure consistency with commercial tutorials.

A second benefit of professionally published training materials is that is easier to ensure consistency throughout the organization. If everyone goes through the same material, they will ultimately share a common set of training and examples. This makes it easier to work through common design exercises or to assume a common basis of understanding when creating organization-specific training materials.

They can be a good basis for in-house training.

Professionally published tutorials can form an excellent basis for in-house training. A more experienced employee can take trainees through the book, using its format as the basis for training sessions. These books are usually broken into self-contained lessons that can be covered in an hour or so, which makes them perfect for both brown-bag sessions and longer training periods that cover several topics at a time.

Publishers generally require a large user base before developing tutorials.

Publishers go through the same calculations about market size and potential sales when considering publication of training materials as they do when considering other types of documentation. Unless they believe there is a user base of at least 50,000 potential readers, of whom 5,000 will purchase the book, they will not go to the effort of creating a book.

About the only downside to commercially published tutorials is actually the opposite of the problems associated with the previous two types of training: Because publishers want to reach the broadest possible audience, books are usually written in a very general manner. If organizationally specific material is needed, it must be created and delivered separately from the printed material.

The tutorials might be too general for the organization's needs.

Option 4: Classroom Training Developed and Delivered by the Open Source Development Team

A few open source product teams that have built businesses based on their product offer formal classroom training. These businesses usually employ the core developers and perhaps a few other individuals who are very knowledgeable about the product. These classes are listed on the project home page and are usually quite easy to find.

The development team might offer classroom training.

There are many positive aspects to this training. First, classroom training is a good way to communicate ideas and explore questions. No training format is better suited to quickly address issues raised by puzzled students. The give-and-take possible with classroom training enables students to focus on their own specific questions.

This is an excellent form of training.

Because the trainer works for the product organization (and is often a key developer of the product), the knowledge level of the instructor is outstanding. Unlike some classroom training situations, where the trainer seems to know less than the students, with developer-led training there is no question about the trainer's level of product knowledge.

The knowledge level of the instructor is outstanding.

Use of a standard training curriculum also ensures a consistent level of knowledge among an organization's employees. This avoids the problem of inconsistent or contradictory training exposure, previously identified as an issue with Web-based examples.

Training consistency is easy to ensure.

The training can be "tuned" for the organization.

Another strength of classroom training is that it can be "tuned" to the organization. If there are specific product functions or features that are critical to the organization, they can be emphasized in the training. Additional training modules that address the organization's needs may be created to supplement the standard modules.

Using this type of training offers other benefits as well.

Finally, having training delivered by the development team offers a significant benefit beyond a good way to train employees. By using a product's development team to train the organization's personnel, a relationship with the developers is established, both personally and financially. If a product is key to an IT organization's success, having an established relationship with the product developers can be a major plus. This relationship can ensure that an organization's problems get priority attention from the developers, which lowers the risk associated with using the product.

This type of training can be expensive.

Of course, there are costs associated with using classroom training. It is expensive, both in direct and indirect costs. The daily rate for an individual to take classroom training can range from $200 to $1,000 per day, so the direct expense of classroom training is quite high. Unless the organization contracts to have the training delivered at a work site, travel expenses can be incurred as well. There are also indirect, or opportunity, costs. Sending someone to a class means that normal work goes unattended or is handled by someone else while they are in class. The power of in-person training must be balanced against the cost of the training itself.

It might not match organizational time frames.

The training schedule might not fit the organization's needs. Training is typically offered only a few times a year, which might not fit the required training schedule. Although a company can mitigate this issue by contracting for custom classes, it can be a problem.

The quality of the training might not be satisfactory.

The quality of the training could be an issue. Open source developers are engineers, not trainers. They might be great at delivering training, but, then again, they might not. Sometimes experts can be the poorest teachers, just as sports superstars are sometimes very poor coaches. Also, not everyone performs at the level of an expert. People who feel left behind by the trainer might not learn very much and could develop a poor attitude about the product they're supposed to be learning about.

Perhaps the biggest issue for this training is its rarity. Only a few open source products have training classes offered by the development organization. Even for those products for which training is available, it is offered only a few times a year. More will be said about the maturity implications of classroom training, but finding this training can be elusive.

It might not be offered often enough.

Option 5: Training Developed and Delivered by Commercial Entities

Commercial training providers step in and create training when there is significant market demand for it. The training can take the form of online tutorials or classroom teaching. Both online and classroom commercial training offer the benefits discussed earlier in the sections on these topics. It should be noted that in the context of this discussion, commercial entities includes both for-profit providers and nonprofit providers like university extension programs, junior colleges, and the like. Both for-profit and nonprofit providers operate with the same motivation, which is to offer training for which significant numbers of students will attend and pay fees. It is relatively easy to find this training via Web searches.

Commercial training entities might offer product training.

Commercial offerings mitigate some of the weaknesses of the training developed and delivered by the open source development team. Training developed by the open source engineers is stronger for being prepared by people who know the product inside out; however, training material prepared by them might be low quality due

It is professionally developed.

to a lack of course development or delivery skills. Commercial training's strengths and weaknesses are the mirror image of those of developer-created training.

It has good course material and pacing.

Commercial training entities are very strong on course development and delivery. They employ experts who are very skilled in creating material that is appropriately paced and progressively more challenging. For classroom training, they employ people who are good communicators and who know how to ensure that all students benefit from the class. On the other hand, their skill level with the software is a question mark that must be answered.

Commercial training has better availability.

Because they are commercial entities, these providers are much more aggressive about making their offerings available. They offer classes more frequently and in more locations. They are very likely to be willing to deliver training on site at a company.

Only the best-established open source products have commercial training available.

In terms of products that have commercial training available, they tend to be the best established. Linux and Apache are by far the most common commercial training offerings, although other products like JBoss and MySQL also have commercial training providers. The distribution of commercial training providers is quite interesting. Training providers are most prevalent in Europe, with a heavy concentration in the United Kingdom. The United States is not nearly as populated with commercial training providers as might be expected given the size of its population and technology industry.

COMMERCIAL TRAINING: ONE OTHER OPTION

One other commercial training alternative might be available to you. If there are commercial products that implement a very similar functionality to the open source product you are using, it might be possible to use the commercial training offerings for those products. It probably wouldn't be possible to attend training offered by a vendor or a vendor-approved training company, but it might be possible to attend a university extension course on the product. The applicability of the commercial product training to the open source product might be as high as 70 or 80 percent. The best bet for this situation is a standards-based product; both the commercial offering and the open source product would deliver very similar functionality, so training for one would apply to the other.

As an example of this, the University of California, Santa Cruz extension program offers a class on "Hands-on OSPF Routing," which uses a Cisco router as the basis for the training. Almost all of the material would be applicable if you were using an open source–based router. Even though the class has a commercial product orientation, you could use it as a training program for your organization's employees as well.

Therefore, if you really want to use commercial training for your employees, be sure to use your imagination to find all the potential options. You might have more possibilities than you think.

Summary of Training Types

Training appears almost as soon as an open source product is available. The ease of Web publishing as well as the enthusiasm of a product's users to share knowledge leads to numerous "minitutorials" spread around the Web. As the user community grows, the creators of the product might develop training to enable less technically oriented users to get up to speed with the product. This usually takes the form of an online tutorial, but if the product developers go forward and create a commercial entity based on their product, the training might be delivered in a classroom format. For the most widely used open source products, commercial entities will deliver training; these entities can be either for-profit or nonprofit.

The form of training available for a product tracks the product maturity.

Assessing Training Maturity

To assess Web-based postings, someone familiar with both the product and the organization's needs should be assigned to do a comprehensive search of the available postings. For the reasons outlined earlier, Web-based postings are unlikely to be comprehensive and

Assign a knowledgeable individual to search for Web-based postings.

therefore are best used as supplements to another training arrangement. Nevertheless, there might be postings that should be part of the training program because they have content particularly appropriate to the organization. The individual assigned to the search should identify valuable postings and collect their links into a centralized document that provides an overview of what each posting provides.

Have two different types of individuals go through the development team's tutorial.

If the open source development team has created a tutorial, a couple of individuals should be assigned to go through the tutorial as a pilot exercise. One should be familiar with the product, and the other should be new to it. The feedback of both individuals will give a full picture of how accurate and useful the tutorial is. If the tutorial feedback is positive, this is excellent news. An online tutorial is a very useful and efficient training mechanism.

Do the same for commercial tutorials.

If no product-team-developed tutorial is available, but a commercial alternative exists, the same process should be followed. It is even more likely that the tutorial will be of high quality, as a professional training organization has developed it.

It's vital to assess classroom training due to its expense.

The remaining alternative is classroom training, either developer delivered or commercially delivered. Because of its costs, both direct and indirect, this is the riskiest training alternative. However, it can be a very powerful way of training employees as well. Therefore, it is important to do a very careful assessment of this alternative before concluding that it is a good choice.

Be sure to check references for the actual trainers.

Ideally, one or more employees should attend the training as a pilot exercise. A range of skills should be represented to enable the organization to get a fully rounded picture of the training program. In this respect, the assessment process is similar to that for online tutorials. However, unlike an online tutorial, the presentation of classroom training can vary enormously, depending on the actual trainer. Consequently, references for classroom training should be checked. The references should cover the training material and the training organization itself. Finally, references for the actual trainers should be checked. At the end of the day, classroom training is delivered by an individual who can make a world of difference in the quality of the teaching. It's not enough to know that the training company is a good one and the class materials are high quality: How good is the person who will be responsible for your employees successfully learning about the product? Check his or her references as well.

At the end of this process, the available training options and their quality can be identified. The organization can assess their quality and plan how employees will be trained on the new product. As has been pointed out a couple of times, a training plan should be part of any product implementation. Failing to plan for training almost ensures that the implementation will be stressful, ragged, and frustrating. It's not worth cutting corners in the training process.

ASSESSING TRAINING: SETTING UP A VPN ON OPENBSD

My firm was asked to do some pro bono work for a local charter high school. Its computing infrastructure is nearly all open source; the sole exception is a commercial education package used to track lesson plans, grades, attendance, and the like. The project we took on was to enable teachers and students to access high school computers from outside locations (primarily their homes). The school's firewall is an OpenBSD box, chosen because it has a good reputation for security. The purpose of the virtual private network (VPN) was to ensure that all communication between the sites was secure. Naturally, we needed to be sure that the existing security was not compromised by the new functionality.

We began a search of the documentation to see if there was a tutorial on setting up a VPN. Although we found reference pages, there was no tutorial. We did a search of the Web to see if anyone had created a tutorial; although we found several examples, none of them were thorough enough for our purposes and each seemed to assume a particular existing configuration (which did not match the school's).

A search of Amazon.com for commercially published books found no good candidates, although one book that will be published shortly looked promising. No table of contents was available to confirm its usefulness, and in any case its availability did not meet our time frame.

The school does not have facilities for a test system; all work would need to be done on the production system. Because of this, we were reluctant to experiment with configuring the VPN via trial and error because making a mistake could expose confidential records to a security breach.

Given all these factors, we decided that trying to use the native VPN capabilities of OpenBSD was not a good option. We therefore decided to purchase a dedicated VPN appliance that could be added with reduced security risk.

From an open source perspective, however, the school continues its commitment. The appliance the school purchased runs an embedded version of Linux to provide VPN services.

This real-world example demonstrates the training assessment process. Because of the risk involved, we needed very specific training materials, but were unable to find them. In their absence, we concluded that moving forward with configuring a native VPN on the OpenBSD firewall would be a poor decision. Our decision nudged us in the direction of purchasing a stand-alone appliance that would be less disruptive to the existing environment and therefore pose less risk.

Assigning a Training Maturity Score

User-generated training indicates a low product maturity level.

User-generated training begins to appear very early in the life of a product, while it is still quite immature. If the only source of training is other users' postings, you can conclude that the product is not very mature. Only one point is assigned if user-generated Web-based training is all that is available. See Table 8.1 for a point assignment breakdown.

Training Type	Maturity Points
Web-based minitutorials	1
Developer-created tutorials	2
Commercial tutorials	3
Classroom delivered by development team	2
Classroom delivered by commercial entity	2
Total training maturity possible score	10

Table 8.1
OSMM Point Assignments for Training

Product developers will create online tutorials when the user community grows and new users begin to use the product. These tutorials are not the same as reference documentation that developers create. Reference documentation is not a learning tool, as anyone who has tried to learn a product by looking at its reference material has discovered. Developers will generally not put together tutorials until the user base is fairly significant. An additional two points are assigned to the product's training maturity score if developer-created tutorials are available.

Developer-created tutorials appear when the user base has grown significantly.

If a commercial entity has created training, it is a strong indication not only that the user base is quite large, but also that the product is being used in commercial environments. This training might be online or in book format, but in either case the fact that a commercial entity has determined that the potential market for product training is large enough to warrant investment in its development means that there is a large audience that will pay for training. This type of training is the first that requires financial investment rather than the time of unpaid volunteers, a strong indication of product maturity. An additional three points are assigned to the training maturity score if commercial training materials are available.

Commercial training indicates significant product maturity.

Classroom training delivered by the product creators or by commercial entities is not very common at this time for most open source products. If classroom training is available, it indicates that the product is extremely mature for the following reason: Classroom

If classroom training is available, it reflects high product maturity.

training is the most expensive form of training available. If organizations are willing to invest in training to the extent of paying for employees to attend classroom training, it indicates that the product is critical to their infrastructure. If other companies have made this level of commitment to the use of the product, it demonstrates that the product is extremely mature.

Developer- and commercially created classroom training indicate a user base willing to pay for training, a sign of significant maturity.

If the development team is delivering classroom training, it shows that the product is so widely used that the developers have been able to start a business on the back of it. For commercial entities to invest in creating classroom training, it means that the demand for it is so high that the development team cannot meet it and there is the opportunity for additional training revenues. Two points are assigned for each type of training, if available.

There are 10 possible points available for training.

Looking at the table, it shows that there is a total of 10 points available for training maturity, with a graduated assignment of points as the form of training becomes more formal and requires financial investment to create.

Assessing JBoss: Training

All five training types are available for JBoss.

All five of the training types possible for open source products are available for JBoss. This is one of the real strengths of the product. The wide availability of training indicates a large user community. In particular, the ready availability of commercial training options, both from the product creators as well as other commercial entities, is a strong positive maturity indicator for JBoss. Please refer to Table 8.2 for the JBoss point assignments based on the following discussion. The checklist used to assess JBoss training options is presented in Table 8.3 on page 180.

Training Type	Maturity Points
Web-based minitutorials	1
Developer-created tutorials	2
Commercial tutorials	1
Classroom delivered by development team	2
Classroom delivered by commercial entity	2
Total training maturity score	8

Table 8.2
JBoss OSMM Point
Assignments for
Training

There are an impressive number of Web-based minitutorials that members of the product community have created and made available. Their quality is quite high, far beyond what one would expect from an immature product. Their comprehensiveness indicates that · users have devoted significant time to attaining JBoss skills. One point is assigned for this item.

There are high-quality Web-based postings available.

The developer-created tutorials are good, although somewhat limited. Early on, JBoss pursued a strategy of making its documentation available for a fee, and developers have concentrated their efforts in that direction. The cost of the fee-based documentation is not very high, so two points are assigned for this item, albeit with the caveat that the tutorials do require a purchase.

Developer-created tutorials are available, but require purchase.

With respect to commercial tutorials, the ones that are available are hard-copy versions of the developer-created online tutorials. It is surprising that there are not several commercial tutorials available; it might be that publishers expect potential readers to refer to general J2EE tutorial materials for learning tools. Because of the paucity of commercial tutorials, only one point is assigned for this item.

Commercial tutorials are not widely available.

JBoss has founded a business on providing services for the namesake J2EE product. Training is one of the most important services and the curriculum demonstrates that. There are four classes

JBoss does make developer-delivered classroom training available.

offered by JBoss, each of which is made available internationally. Therefore, two points are assigned for this item.

Many commercial providers offer classroom training as well.

There are also a large number of other commercial entities that provide training on the JBoss product. Some are certified by JBoss; others have set up shop and announced that they are capable of training. A careful assessment of which provider to use is necessary for anyone considering using commercial training. Nonetheless, because training is provided by so many entities, two points are assigned for this item.

JBoss is assigned 8 out of 10 possible training maturity points.

Because there are so many options for obtaining training on the JBoss product, it receives a score of 8 out of a possible 10 points for training. Any organization considering using JBoss as an open source product can feel comfortable that its employees will find good training options. This does not obviate the need for assessing which options are actually used, but the high maturity score for this element indicates that obtaining high-quality training should be easily accomplished.

Table 8.3   OSMM Training Assessment Checklist

OPEN SOURCE MATURITY MODEL Training Assessment Checklist	
Product Name: JBoss	
Method	**Notes**
Web-Based Minitutorials	
Did Web search for three different JBoss product aspects: deployment descriptors, Container Managed Persistence, and Java Message Service.	Found significant numbers of Web minitutorials on all three subjects (including several full-blown tutorials). Review of material found it to be of high quality and accurate.

Table 8.3   OSMM Training Assessment Checklist *(cont.)*

Method	Notes
Developer-Created Tutorials	
Searched JBoss site.	JBoss.org offers free "Getting Started" document; other documentation that is tutorial-flavored is available for sale at nominal prices at JBoss.com.
Reviewed documentation for quality and thoroughness.	Documentation covers all relevant areas of JBoss and J2EE. Because J2EE is a standard, other books are available to train on general subject.
Commercial Tutorials	
Searched JBoss site as well as Amazon.com.	There are commercially published versions of the material available for sale on the JBoss.com site; see notes for Developer-Created Tutorials.
Classroom Delivered by Development Team	
Reviewed JBoss.org and JBoss.com sites.	This is a major revenue generator for JBoss.com. Four classes are offered: Introduction to JBoss Advanced Development with JBoss JBoss Administrator Training JBoss Bootcamp
Contacted three customers for references on training.	Positive feedback. Only criticism is that training is not offered as frequently as would be convenient. Customers felt it was a significant advantage to have actual developers delivering training.
Classroom Delivered by Commercial Entity	
Reviewed JBoss.com site for certified training by partners.	Found page listing classes, dates, city, and training partner delivering training. Four different partners delivering training. Classes offered are: J2EE on JBoss Training JBoss Administration
Did Web search to locate other training providers not listed by JBoss.	Found at least 10 other companies that provide JBoss training, located throughout the world. Most appear to have been training on JBoss one year or less. Similar curriculums; most classes appear to cover in one extended class several of the classes offered by JBoss itself.

Table 8.3   OSMM Training Assessment Checklist *(cont.)*

Method	Notes
Classroom Delivered by Commercial Entity *(cont.)*	
Spoke to several of the other JBoss training providers to determine quality.	These providers are mostly system integrators that also provide training. Highly technical trainers, good source for high-bandwidth knowledge transfer. Potential issue in training materials quality, as these materials appear to have been developed without JBoss's direct involvement. If any of these providers is considered for training, materials must be reviewed and ideally an employee sent through for pilot purposes.

9

Open Source Integration with Other Products

Executive Summary

No man is an island, and no software operates on its own. Even stand-alone products run in an operating system environment. Integrating a new software product into the existing software infrastructure is one of the most important—and challenging—tasks that an IT organization must address with a new software product.

Integrating open source products can be even more challenging due to their unique characteristics. This chapter outlines the challenges in integrating open source products into an existing software stack and the options an organization has available to reduce the risk associated with the integration. It addresses the reasons why commercial software vendors often delay creating integrations with open source products, and discusses how to motivate commercial vendors to create needed integrations. It further describes the opportunities to bypass these issues by using the new Web services integration model. The chapter closes by assessing the maturity implications of the integrations available for an open source product and the integration maturity score for JBoss, our example OSMM product.

Software stack is a term that depicts the conceptual model that many people use for their software infrastructure. A software stack portrays a layered collection of software, each resting on one or more lower pieces of software, and each having one or more software products resting on it. Every piece of software in the stack consumes services from the software below it and delivers services to the software above it.

What this means is that every piece of software has to work cooperatively with other software. This working together, called *integration,* reflects the modern software infrastructure of enterprises. Any new piece of software has to find its place in the software stack and be able to work with the software products that already exist in the stack.

A primary motivation for using open source software is to replace currently existing applications in the software stack. By replacing expensive commercial software with open source products, the organization reduces its cost structure, freeing up capital for investment in other areas.

For a new product to succeed as part of the software stack, it must integrate seamlessly with the existing components of the stack. Any product introduced into a company's application infrastructure will face integration challenges, but open source products face additional challenges that are discussed next. For an open source implementation to succeed, all integrations that a product requires must be available; otherwise, the implementation will be difficult or impossible.

Integration: The Hidden Achilles Heel

IT environments require large numbers of software products to work cooperatively.

Today's IT organizations run complex shops. The average company has more than 100 software products simultaneously running, each providing one or more services. The computing infrastructure of most companies is a complicated arrangement of software products, each performing its function, but also working cooperatively with others in a network of data feeds, RPCs, and direct application integration. Figure 9.1 depicts a typical software stack for an IT organization. It is easy to see that every piece of the stack has to interoperate with a number of other software products.

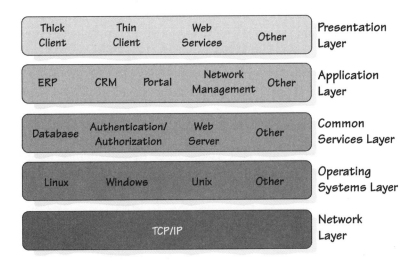

Figure 9.1
Typical Software Stack

Therefore, choosing a product for implementation in an organization's software infrastructure involves not just assessing whether it provides the desired functionality; it also requires assessing whether it can be integrated with the existing infrastructure components.

Any new product must fit into the existing environment.

The challenges of software integration have increased as IT organizations have moved away from product suites to best-of-breed solutions, achieving better functionality at the cost of more complex infrastructure. As additional products are installed to provide functionality, business requirements dictate that they do not act in isolation, but that they share their data. Only by being able to access all data in a seamless fashion can the company take a 360-degree view of its key success factors. Companies simply must be able to create a comprehensive view of all of the data residing in their applications within the firewall.

The move to best-of-breed products has increased integration challenges.

Moreover, companies are now facing new integration challenges as they recognize that they must reach across their firewall to integrate with other organizations like suppliers, customers, logistics partners, and outsourced service providers. The push to optimize

The move to supply chain integration has increased these challenges as well.

supply chains has created a new class of integration needs and made it even more critical that software applications be easily integrated as they are installed in the organization's software stack. The increased requirement for integration makes the ability of new players to integrate into the software stack critical.

Challenges of Integration

There are many challenges to successful integration.

Integration is vitally important when considering an addition to the organization's software stack, a significant challenge. There are a number of reasons why successful integrations fail, but the primary reason is that planning for necessary integrations is put off until the last minute—or even beyond the last minute, as in, "It's in production, where's the report we always get every morning?" The topic of integration is so important that it must be addressed early in the software selection process, which is why integration planning was addressed in Chapter 5, "The Open Source Product." Identifying all necessary integrations must be part of planning for an open source product implementation. However, even with a rigorous planning process, there are still potential problems with the integration process and reasons why necessary software integrations might have been missed:

- The system's documentation might be out of date. New pieces of software might have been added but never documented. In the heat of battle, many things that should be done aren't, and system documentation is a frequent casualty.
- Key personnel most familiar with the system might no longer be with the organization. They might have left or, as has been the case recently, downsized in a cost-reduction campaign. The organizational memory that could have been drawn on during the planning process is incomplete.
- Integrations between software products might have been done without the organization's awareness. Vendor personnel

or consultants might have created a data transfer capability or installed additional software—all without telling the IT organization. Creating documentation at the end of a professional services engagement is often promised by the salesperson; the person doing the work often is pressured to get on to the next engagement or is indifferent to the benefits of documentation. So documentation for work done on the organization's behalf might not have been completed.

Each of these reasons could cause the planning process to fail to identify all necessary integrations. However, because some product integrations might be difficult to identify does not constitute a reason to shortcut the process. It's far better to miss just one than to not document six or seven that can be identified.

Planning is key to success.

Challenges of Open Source Integration

Open source software poses additional challenges in identifying and confirming the existence of all required integrations. Many times integration is necessary between an open source product and a commercial product. For a number of reasons, the commercial product provider might not be motivated to integrate or even to certify that an existing integration is a supported configuration.

Open source increases the challenge of integration.

This situation frequently occurred while Linux was proving itself as a production-ready platform. Commercial providers were reluctant to port their products to Linux, reasoning that it wasn't worth the bother for a "hobbyist" platform.

Commercial providers first considered open source "hobbyist" software.

Although Linux has proved its mettle in production environments and many commercial software vendors have moved their applications to Linux, this situation still occurs with other open source products. A commercial vendor will be aware of an open source product that could integrate with the company's products, but won't consider it worth the time to do the work.

Despite the success of Linux, other open source products are still deprecated.

OpenLDAP can serve as an example of the open source integration challenge.

As an example, imagine that an IT organization wished to implement OpenLDAP in its software stack, as a mechanism to access its authentication/authorization directory (see Figure 9.2 for a graphical representation). For the organization to successfully implement the product, it must be able to integrate all products that consume these security services with OpenLDAP. If any of the existing applications has no means to integrate with OpenLDAP, there will be a significant problem. Even if there is a way to integrate a product with OpenLDAP, if the vendor does not certify it as supported, there can be problems.

Figure 9.2
OpenLDAP Integration Challenge

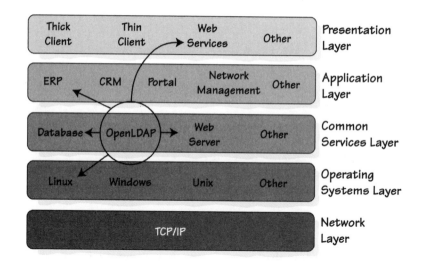

The anonymity of open source usage increases the challenge.

The anonymous, noncommercial nature of open source exacerbates this situation. If the new product were itself a commercial product, the IT organization could lobby someone to get the work done. If the need to integrate with an existing product were holding up the sale, someone at the new product's company would push to get the integration done.

For an open source product, that motivation doesn't exist. There is no sales rep to negotiate with the existing product's business development group. Open source providers don't have anyone who can push a commercial vendor to perform an integration—the open source business model lacks the revenue to support business development activities. In fact, because of the anonymous nature of open source downloading, the development team might be completely unaware that integration with another product is necessary.

The open source development team might not even be aware of the need for integration.

Therefore, there might be additional challenges in integrating open source products beyond those present in any software integration. This might seem like cause for despair, but in fact integration challenges for commercial and open source software are being reduced dramatically by the rise of new standards in the computing environment.

There is hope, however, with the rise of new standards.

New Standards in Integration

Although integrations are a necessary and challenging issue for IT organizations, they are far less onerous today than they would have been even three years ago. In the recent past, each integration project had to be handled as a one-off project, requiring custom integration products that imposed proprietary application programming interfaces (APIs) to link applications. Every product that needed to share data with another would require an analysis of its data structures, any available APIs it offered, and then a plan of attack to create a method to retrieve data from the product. That was for one side of the integration. Naturally, there was another product on the other side that required a similar planning process. Once that was done, a third plan had to be created to identify how the data would be transported, which required working with a third set of programming interfaces in an integration product (typically quite expensive and complex).

In the past, product integration was an enormous technical challenge.

A product integration project went like this:

1. Identify the data needed from product 1. Develop a strategy to retrieve it either via product-specific APIs or, even worse, to extract the data from the native store (usually a relational database). Retrieving from the native store is dangerous, as this might bypass necessary workflow or data integrity functionality, but sometimes this is the only mechanism possible. Create an interface for the product to retrieve the data necessary for integration.
2. Repeat step 1 for product 2, including creating another API.
3. Write a product-1-to-product-2–specific transport using one of the numerous complicated integration products offering message queue or publish/subscribe interfaces.
4. Pray that none of the products changes. If one does, repeat steps 1 through 3.

Because of the difficulty and cost, only a few integrations were attempted.

It's easy to see why only the most critical integration projects were ever contemplated. Integration the old way was complex, expensive, and protracted—when it succeeded at all. Many product integrations with real business benefits—sharing data between a company's order entry system and its customer relationship management system, for example—weren't done at all. Few companies had employees with the necessary skills to perform this work; most of the rest just couldn't afford it.

The rise of XML has reduced the cost and complexity dramatically.

The situation is dramatically different today. In the past few years new standards have emerged that make integration faster, simpler, and cheaper. The first standard, Extensible Markup Language (XML), provides an easy way to represent data in a human-readable format. In the past, data was extracted in the native format of each of the endpoint applications and then translated into the proprietary integration mechanism's data format. Each integration interface translated the data it received from the integration mechanism into its native data representation. This three-step translation process had to be manually created by a project team member, and, as you might expect, was very difficult, requiring significant technical expertise.

Perhaps even worse, however, was that the data was transmitted in a binary format. This format could not easily read by humans, making debugging extremely challenging. Debugging integration applications required reading a dump of the data (if the engineer was experienced enough to do so), or using yet another application that could read the dump and present the data in human-readable form. Using XML changed all that; data is transmitted in human-readable form and is accompanied by a tag that describes it. It is quite easy to read through an XML data stream and see what data elements are present and what the value of each element is.

XML makes debugging an integration far easier.

So, XML addressed the integration challenge of formatting the data by offering a standard way to represent data that could be processed by software applications as well as read by humans. This represents a huge advance over the previous methods of representing data.

XML has nearly solved the integration data representation issue.

However, this advance in data representation does not address the other part of the integration challenge—extracting and transmitting the data. Even with standardized ways to represent the data payload, it still remained difficult to create the integration mechanism. Fortunately, a new standard based on XML and standard Internet protocols is available to address the integration challenge: Web services.

Web services addresses the other part of the challenge: extraction and transmission of data.

Web services substitutes standard Web transport protocols for the previous proprietary transport mechanisms. The most common protocol used to date is Hypertext Transfer Protocol (HTTP), the standard protocol for serving Web pages. This is very handy, as most IT infrastructures have Web servers installed. Therefore, it is not usually necessary to require a new software application to enable

Standard protocols are used for Web services data transmission.

basic Web services connectivity: The integration can ride on an already existing connectivity mechanism. There are other protocols that Web services can use as well, including Simple Mail Transport Protocol (SMTP). By far the most typical arrangement, however, is to use HTTP.

Web services also uses XML to represent the integration services themselves.

The genius of Web services does not stop with a convenient transport mechanism and the use of XML as the payload, however. It actually uses XML to represent the integration services themselves, providing a standardized way for applications to offer their data for use by other applications. At a stroke, Web services has vastly reduced the complexity of application integration.

Web services are the de facto standard for future product integration.

Web services has rapidly become the format for the next generation of application integration. Most software applications deliver Web services integration points as part of their product to make sharing data easier. The vendors of software infrastructure products like J2EE application servers have added functionality to make it easy to expose Enterprise JavaBean functionality as a Web service. And, as you might expect, there are a large number of open source tools to create Web services interfaces for applications. Chapter 5, "The Open Source Product," presented some information on SOAP::Lite, a Perl Web services module that our firm used for a middleware solution. It went into production approximately six months ago and has performed flawlessly ever since.

WEB SERVICES: HOPE OR HYPE?

The importance of the Web services revolution can be demonstrated by one example. In 2002, Merrill Lynch developed an integration project plan to offer access to legacy systems. Instead of using the proprietary integration product they had been planning on, they decided to offer the integration endpoints via Web services as an experiment. Their experiment succeeded beyond their wildest hopes. Not only were they successful in opening up their legacy systems with Web services interfaces, but the project took only three months rather than the full year their plan called for. The highlight of the project was the financial savings. Rather than the $800,000 Merrill had budgeted for the integration project, the Web services version cost them only $30,000, a savings of 96 percent—made possible, in part, by the use of open source Web services software.

How Integration Standards Help Open Source

Clearly, Merrill Lynch's experience demonstrates the power and cost-effectiveness of Web services. However, this is a book about open source. Why are Web services important to the topic of open source integration? As more applications offer Web services interfaces and Web services toolkits enable building Web services interfaces inexpensively, the challenge of integrating open source within the IT software stack diminishes.

How do Web services interact with open source?

Although many commercial product companies might not feel it is worthwhile to create an integration with an open source product, if, as is likely, they create a general Web services interface, it can be used as an integration point for an open source product. The problem of getting the attention of the vendor is bypassed by the availability of an easy integration mechanism for their product.

As a de facto standard, Web services makes it much easier to integrate open source products with commercial software.

What this means for organizations considering open source is that one of the most critical and difficult issues—integration within the software stack—is becoming far less onerous. If a necessary integration with a commercial product is not available, an IT organization has an alternative: It can affordably create integration by using Web services interfaces.

Open source integration has become much easier.

As Web services become ubiquitous, the possibility of being stranded by a missing necessary integration between an open source product and a commercial product is rapidly being reduced. Even if a necessary integration is not available, the organization has a realistic option to create one.

Organizations can use Web services to replace missing product integration.

Defining Integration Requirements

Identifying
required
integrations is
crucial.

Clearly, identifying or creating the necessary integrations is critical for introducing a new product into an organization's software stack. If the new product is open source, the task might be further complicated by the lack of available integrations with commercial products that are already present in the software stack.

The best approach to successfully integrate an open source product into your software stack is to plan for it and create a process to ensure it is accomplished successfully.

Identify the Needed Integrations

Starting early
reduces
integration risk.

It is no accident that this topic was addressed in the very first step of the open source product selection process outlined in Chapter 5, "The Open Source Product." Starting early offers the only realistic hope of successfully meeting the integration challenge. An early start allows for the inevitable delays and offers enough time for any necessary integration engineering work.

System
documentation is
the first place to
look.

The identification process begins by looking at any available system documentation for identified integrations. Of course, as noted earlier, system documentation is often out of date or incomplete, so this is just the first place to look.

Members of the
team should be
queried for their
knowledge about
existing
integrations.

Product selection team members should be asked about any product integrations they are aware of. System administration or operations personnel might have better knowledge of how the software stack actually operates, as opposed to the less realistic notions of individuals further removed from the front line.

Look at the
outputs of the
system for clues to
unknown
integrations.

Operations personnel are not infallible in their knowledge, however. They might not be aware of software running on a system that has been placed there by inside or outside personnel. So the next task in step 1 is to take a look at the outputs of the system to determine if they indicate a blended data source. Reports that correlate two disparate types of data are good indicators of an underlying integration.

Another good place to look for additional integration activities is in the list of processes running on systems. There might be processes that have "tip-off" names that indicate an unknown integration.

Examine the system process tables.

Obviously, this process is much easier if an open source product is replacing an existing application. In this case, one would hope that all necessary integrations are documented or discoverable through process table inspection. If the open source product is not replacing another, but is brand new, the effort to identify necessary integrations will be more difficult as they will need to be designed rather than merely discovered. In this case, more emphasis will be needed on the up-front planning described in Chapter 5, "The Open Source Product." However, it is always more difficult to foresee needed product functionality than to describe existing functionality, so the product team should be prepared to be surprised with new requirements as the process unfolds. The emphasis on product requirement planning reduces to a minimum the downstream surprises.

If the open source product is a new installation rather than a replacement the task might be more difficult.

Locating Resources

For the product elements discussed in previous chapters, locating resources was a relatively painless task that required looking at the product Web site, doing some Web searches, and perhaps querying the user community. Because integrations are so organization-specific, locating resources requires more work, as well as recognizing that the task will inevitably be organization-specific, because every organization's software stack is unique. Locating integration resources for a particular organization requires a three-step process:

Locating resources is a three-step process.

1. Identify existing integrations.
2. Create an integration plan for missing integration mechanisms.
3. Identify any integrations that cannot be created.

Identify Existing Integrations

See if existing integrations will work with the new open source product.

The first step is to review each of the existing integrations to determine whether they will work with the new open source product. If you are lucky, each of them will work satisfactorily with the new product and you can skip the next step. If you are not so lucky, there will be one or more integration mechanisms that will not work with the new product and they should be identified so that alternatives can be developed. Lest this effort seem like overkill, it is no more than should be done for any new product that is a candidate for the software stack. Open source does not change this fact. What is different is that some commercial vendors, out of disinterest or disbelief in the potential of open source, might not have created integrations with an open source product, while making one available for an alternative commercial product.

Create an Integration Plan for Missing Integration Mechanisms

Missing integrations should be placed on a short list of work items.

There should now be a short list of necessary integrations that do not have native mechanisms to accomplish the task. By native mechanisms, I mean some way to accomplish the mechanism that does not require engineering effort. If two applications, one an existing part of the software stack and the other an open source candidate for the stack, can exchange data immediately or as a result of some configuration work, the integration is trivial and can be considered native.

If, on the other hand, there is no existing integration mechanism, and an engineering effort will be required, that integration should go on the short list of to-do projects that is part of the overall plan.

There are two approaches for obtaining needed integrations with commercial software: cajole and build. Which of the two approaches is most appropriate depends on how urgently the solution is needed and the ability of the organization to influence the commercial software provider.

There are two options for obtaining commercial software integrations.

The cajole alternative involves convincing the commercial provider it should create an integration with the open source product in question. Some items of influence that might be brought to bear include (in increasing order of likelihood of achieving the desired effect):

You can lobby the commercial vendor.

- Convincing the provider that it's the right thing to do. Once in a while vendors will do things they should in the spirit of cooperation for the greater good of the technology industry. It doesn't happen very often, but it could be your lucky day.
- Demonstrating that the desired integration will be a common requirement for many IT organizations. The provider will come under increasing pressure from many customers to provide it. Strength in numbers is a cliché, but showing that a number of the provider's customers will request this integration demonstrates that it's in the provider's self-interest to create one.
- Being a significantly large customer of the provider that you can directly influence them. If your company buys a lot of product from the provider, or you influence the purchase of a lot of product (for example, if you are a consulting firm that recommends products), you have a much higher probability of motivating the provider to create the needed integration.
- Funding the integration. If the commercial software provider agrees that the first two alternatives demonstrate that they should do the integration, but they can't justify doing so, the offer to fund all or part of the effort might do the trick. Whether this alternative is possible depends on your budget and how important the integration is.

Building the
integrations
yourself is the
second option.

The build alternative requires the organization to take on some amount of engineering work to create the missing integration(s). By now, you should have a list of needed integrations that must be implemented so that the open source product can take its place in the organization's software stack.

Creating these integrations involves working through the following process:

- Determine the right mechanism for each integration. There might be a choice of several options that will each successfully accomplish the integration, but the amount of work required for each one could vary significantly. Another factor in choosing an integration mechanism is how robust the resulting integration will be. An implementation option that might be fragile—prone to crashing, requiring lots of administrative attention, or even just difficult to assess whether or not it's working—could eliminate it as a good choice.
- Determine who is going to create the integration mechanism selected in step 1. Part of your decision process is the skill sets you have in house. It's usually cheaper to use internal personnel for engineering. In the Merrill Lynch example presented in the sidebar earlier, a significant part of the savings was realized by using employees rather than consultants to do the integration work. Whether created by someone within the organization or an outside service provider, a budget assessment should be made. How much will the integration cost?
- Develop a schedule for each integration. When will it be ready? This needs to be mapped into the overall project plan to assure that the resulting schedule still meets the organization's needs. If not, step 2 needs to be revisited to see if another option is available.

- Make a final selection for each integration. Document the selection and put it into the project plan.

Identify Any Integrations That Cannot Be Created

It could be that despite all efforts, it is impossible for you to obtain the necessary product integrations. Perhaps a key commercial product does not offer a native integration with the open source product and also has no general integration mechanisms. Despite efforts to entice the vendor to create an integration, it proves unwilling to do so. Furthermore, there might be no way to create an integration by way of direct database calls, APIs or Web services. Or possibly, an integration might be feasible, but not in the time frame needed or within the available budget. It is, as they say, a dead end.

It might not be possible to obtain all needed integrations.

If this is the case, the organization has two courses of action available to it.

First, it might conclude that, lacking the necessary integration(s), the open source product under consideration is not appropriate. The lacking integrations create an insurmountable barrier to using the product. If that is the case, this product cannot be used in the organization's software stack. It is better realize this while the effort is still a paper assessment or, at worst, a pilot project, rather than discovering it as the new product is rolled into production.

You can choose to discontinue your efforts with the product.

There might be other open source products that could provide the necessary functionality that can now be considered and assessed. If a short list was created during the product functionality assessment phase, it's simply a matter of moving down to the next most attractive alternative and performing an assessment on that product. If this integration assessment phase has indicated that it is likely to be challenging for any product, it might be appropriate to move the integration assessment phase earlier in the overall assessment of the newly selected product for consideration.

Another product from the original short list might be an option.

You might decide
to move forward
despite the
missing
integrations.

The second course of action is to recognize that the necessary integration(s) will not be available, at least in the necessary time frame, and decide to go ahead with selecting the product nonetheless. If it is vital to get the new product into place, it might be worth living with diminished integration functionality. The required integration might be available later, so moving forward with the product makes sense because the situation is not permanent. This product option might be the best available and all other options have even greater drawbacks. The missing integrations cause this product to be the least objectionable alternative.

At the end of this step, if your organization decides to move forward with an open source product knowing that it lacks some integration capabilities, it will be a conscious decision and not an accidental situation that will cause pain and recriminations later.

ENSURING INTEGRATIONS WORK PROPERLY: USING A PILOT PROJECT

The topic of integrations is difficult because, as described earlier, some necessary integrations might remain unknown even with the best of intentions. Integrations might have been created by people who prepared no documentation and are no longer available to question. Possibly outside personnel created one or more integrations and did not bother to tell anyone who worked for the organization—the integration is there and working but no one knows about it. On the other hand, if the organization decides to create an integration, there is a question about how well the new code will work in production—and production is the wrong place to find out it doesn't work! Each of these situations highlights the problem of moving a product directly into production without testing it.

A pilot project is a low-risk, relatively inexpensive way to confirm that the product will work in production and that all potential issues have been identified and addressed. Every product that will form an important part of an organization's software stack should be exercised in a pilot environment prior to being installed in production.

A pilot environment should mirror your production environment as closely as possible. It might not be possible to exactly re-create the production environment, but a production-like setup should be established. The reasons the production environment cannot be re-created vary: The production environment might have too high a level of transactions to be economically re-created due to hardware constraints; the software to drive complex interactions that mimic real-world customer use might be unavailable or prohibitively expensive; or perhaps personnel are not available to perform the work necessary for a production-mirrored test environment.

Notwithstanding these issues, a pilot environment can be created so that typical transactions and workloads can be modeled to ensure that the candidate open source product works properly. A pilot project also offers the opportunity for personnel to get better acquainted with the product in a less hectic atmosphere.

A pilot installation that mirrors production use also will flush out any integrations that are necessary but missing. If a daily report that always shows up doesn't, it's clear that something's not right. It is far better to discover it at this stage rather than when the missing functionality could cause real business pain.

Assessing Source Integration Maturity

Assessing the maturity implications of the commercial product integrations with an open source product can be difficult. Because many commercial vendors will not be aware of the number of installations of an open source product due to user anonymity, the absence of a native integration performed by the vendor does not necessarily imply that the open source product is immature. It could just mean that the vendor is not especially attuned to open source users and might not be aware of the size of the product's installed base.

Missing integrations do not necessarily imply an immature product.

On the other hand, if a commercial vendor has performed an integration, that is a strong sign of the open source product's maturity. The vendor wouldn't have performed the work unless it was convinced that there is a significant installed base of the open source

Commercial vendor integrations are a strong sign of product maturity.

product, sufficient in size to impact the sales of the vendor's product if no integration is possible.

Community-created integrations are also a sign of product maturity.

Alternatively, if someone in the open source community has created an integration to one of the commercial products in your software stack, it indicates that the open source product is being used in a production environment similar to yours. This is also a strong sign of maturity.

The percentage of existing needed integrations is a good indicator of maturity.

A rough way to assess the maturity level of the integration element is to calculate how many of the necessary product integrations are actually available without needing any work on your part. If the available integrations comprise a large percentage of the total needed, it indicates significant maturity for the open source product in question.

Assigning an Integration Maturity Score

The potential integration point score is 10.

We have identified several integration mechanisms in this chapter. Each of them has maturity implications for any given open source product. Table 9.1 contains the possible scores for each integration item. Based on a possible point total of 10, the scoring is as follows:

- If the necessary integrations have been identified through the process outlined in this chapter, two points are assigned, as this is the first step toward integration success.
- If there are integrations that need to be developed and it is possible to do them using established standards like Web services, an additional three points are assigned.
- Finally, if there are integrations that are necessary requiring one or more commercial vendors to create custom integrations and those integrations are available or are under development, or there are integrations available created by other product users, an additional five points are assigned to

reflect the fact that the open source product demonstrates significant maturity. This maturity is demonstrated by the fact that a commercial vendor has concluded that the investment in creating an integration is worthwhile, a strong indicator that the open source product is widely used by customers with money to invest.

Maturity Element	Score
Integrations identified	2
Necessary integrations possible via self-development	3
Necessary integrations developed by commercial vendors	5
Integration maturity possible score	10

Table 9.1
Integration Maturity Score

Assessing JBoss: Integration

Integrating a new open source product into the existing software stack is vitally important. However, it is also organization-specific. Each company has its own software infrastructure into which the new product must be integrated. For that reason, the OSMM integration maturity example described here reflects an idealized software stack. This example is used to demonstrate the process that would be used for a real-world software infrastructure. Therefore, the evaluation methods identified in the Integration Assessment Checklist (see Table 9.3) document the basic process used for an integration assessment. In your actual use of the checklist, each method would probably have a number of notes, reflecting your findings during system documentation review, interviews, and machine process examination. See Table 9.3 for the evaluation methods available for integrations.

Integration requirements are organization-specific.

We give full marks to JBoss. (See Table 9.2 for the example scoring.) Integration is one of JBoss's real strengths. It is bundled as part of a number of commercial products, it offers several integration

JBoss has excellent integration capabilities.

mechanisms as part of its J2EE conformance (including both Web services and Java Message Service (JMS), and a number of commercial software vendors certify their product as working with JBoss. Naturally, if you were doing an actual assessment of JBoss, you would need to evaluate how well it integrates with the products operating in your software infrastructure, and the score for this element might not be as high as in this example.

Table 9.2
JBoss Integration
Maturity Score

Maturity Element	Score
Integrations identified	2
Necessary integrations possible via self-development	3
Necessary integrations developed by commercial vendors	5
Integration maturity score	10

Table 9.3   OSMM Integration Assessment Checklist

OPEN SOURCE MATURITY MODEL	
Integration Assessment Checklist	
Product Name: JBoss	
Method	**Notes**
Integrations Identified	
Reviewed all applicable system documentation.	Two integrations documented: 1. JMS used to exchange data with existing inventory system. 2. EJB calls to ecommerce database.
Interviewed members of product selection task force to determine needed product integrations.	None identified beyond two listed in system documentation.
Interviewed development and operations personnel to uncover any undocumented integrations.	Additional use of JMS to push data to partner portal.
Reviewed process tables/Task Manager process list to see if any integration processes can be identified.	None identified as a result of this step.

Table 9.3   OSMM Integration Assessment Checklist *(cont.)*

Method	Notes
Integrations Identified *(cont.)*	
Identified any additional integrations required through discussion with task force members, development and operations personnel, and any other affected parties.	None identified as a result of this step.
Necessary Integrations Available via Self-Development	
Identified missing integrations.	None missing.
Evaluated possible integration mechanisms that can be used to create necessary integrations.	Ecommerce application offers Web services interface that can be used to replace direct database calls. Will be explored as to viability.
Necessary Integrations Developed by Commercial Vendors	
Identified missing integrations.	Partner portal commercial product offers Web services interface. Will assess functionality and performance during pilot test.
Determined commercial integrations that are available.	None missing.
Necessary Integrations That Are Not Available	
Identified any integrations that cannot be created via previous four mechanisms.	None missing.
For every missing integration, decided whether project can go forward without integration.	Not applicable for this assessment.

10

Open Source Professional Services

Executive Summary

To this point, we have assessed a product's maturity by looking at the product itself and at how it can integrate into an organization's software stack. In this chapter, we turn our focus away from product-specific elements to focus on an increasingly important factor in software implementation: professional services.

Many IT organizations rely extensively on professional services organizations. They are used if the organization does not have sufficient resources to implement a project or lacks specific technical skills. Today, many IT organizations have moved to being very lean in terms of headcount; for them, using services firms is not a temporary engagement but is, instead, a way of keeping running expenses down.

In locating and using professional services firms for open-source–oriented projects, IT organizations will need to be creative. The large, well-known firms have not embraced open source (other than Linux) to this point, so it might not be possible to rely on the "brand name" firms. There are firms that focus on open source, but for the most part they are small and not well established. This means that organizations seeking services will need to be persistent as well as selective in their assessment when locating potential services partners.

This chapter provides an overview of open source and professional services, discusses how to locate services firms, and describes how to assess the quality of the services available for an open source product. The chapter closes with a maturity assessment of the professional services for our example product, JBoss.

Open Source Professional
Services Overview

This chapter focuses on pure services firms.

Although we have discussed services several times thus far in the book, it has always been in the context of an open source company that provides consulting as part of its business. In this chapter, the focus is on companies whose raison d'être is providing professional services. You might know them as consulting firms or system integrators. They are part of the huge business of helping companies solve their IT problems. Well-known professional services firms include Accenture, IBM Global Services, and EDS. However, these are the giants in the field. Professional service firms range from tiny to enormous, from actual mom-and-pop operations all the way to globe-straddling behemoths.

Services firms sell time and expertise.

What they all have in common is that they are services firms. They make their living by selling the time and expertise of their employees to clients. Professional services firms are problem solvers that sell their services. What this implies, of course, is that they must keep their people busy to be successful. For professional services firms, time—literally—is money.

The availability of professional services is a strong open source product maturity indicator.

The availability of professional services for an open source product carries strong implications for its maturity. To understand why this is so, it is important to understand how professional services firms operate.

Professional services firms require significant demand before beginning a new practice area.

A significant investment is required for a firm to offer a new practice area (*practice* being the term used to describe an offering based on a particular product or product area; for example, many services firms have a customer relationship management practice). Beyond the obvious costs of training personnel on the new product and procuring new software and hardware, there are a number of soft costs as well. Forming a relationship with the software partner takes time and money, as does the marketing effort required to make potential clients aware of the new practice. Also, early engagements in the practice tend to be lower margin as employees learn how to implement the product in real-world settings.

Because of these very large expenses, service firms only begin a new practice area when they are convinced there is significant client demand for the products. In short, service firms only invest when they are sure their investment will be paid back many times over.

Open Source and Professional Services

Because of the commitment of large technology companies to Linux, the large system integrators have developed Linux-oriented service offerings. It's natural that if IBM and Hewlett-Packard are emphasizing Linux to their customer base that the large integrators would develop expertise on the platform. However, to date, the large professional services firms are not yet focused on other open source products.

To date, Linux has been the focus of major professional services firms.

The largest firms are waiting to see stronger evidence that their customers are ready to implement open source software and require help doing so. You might say that the large firms are a trailing indicator of open source maturity, as they require very significant demand before they will commit the resources needed for a new service line. However, it is probable that in the near future the well-known national and international firms will begin to offer open source–based consulting.

Services firms are waiting to see stronger demand before developing service areas for other open source products.

This does not mean that there are no open source professional services available today. Smaller local and regional firms do offer open source–focused professional services. These companies often are more technically focused and might have been started by open source enthusiasts. Their employees tend to be more technically

There are local and regional professional services firms available.

focused than those at the larger firms, so they might be more interested in open source and willing to work with it.

Open source is well-suited to these firms' customer base.

Another reason smaller firms offer open source–based services has to do with their client base. They tend to sell to small- and medium-sized businesses that have a strong cost awareness in all aspects of their business, including IT. Because their clients operate on tight budgets, these firms often have to use open source products in their projects. Based on this, they will develop expertise in open source software and focus on it as a specialty.

Your service provider will probably be a local or regional firm.

This means that if you want to work with a system integrator for an open source–based project, you will probably need to work with a smaller, specialized firm. Depending on the scope of the project, it might be necessary to bring in more than one firm, as a single firm might not have expertise on all the open source products used for the project.

Defining Professional Services Requirements

Using professional services firms is an excellent choice for the following situations:

- Your organization is shorthanded at the moment but will have internal expertise on hand in the future. An integrator can be used to take on specific project tasks while the hiring organization prepares for its future commitment.
- You plan to use the service engagement in part as a way to train your staff on the new product. Knowledge transfer can be excellent using experienced service personnel as project leads or mentors.
- You do not plan to employ internal expertise, but do plan to use this firm or another services firm as a long-term partner to provide ongoing support for the application.

However, using a services firm on a short-term basis to create an application without some kind of long-term plan is a risky situation. Having experts create a solution that is "dropped off" afterward with someone who doesn't understand it leaves the organization exposed if (or when) the application crashes.

You should define your professional services requirements in light of the foregoing. It is important to keep in mind all of the different groups that will be involved with the application throughout its life. It could be that your organization does not have development personnel available, but that your operations group will be responsible for ongoing support and maintenance. Therefore, you might consider using an outside firm to develop the application, but give internal resources day-to-day responsibility for it. In that case, your services plan should include complete project documentation, formal handover milestones, and an escalation mechanism.

Locating Resources

Despite the fact that it's primarily smaller firms that focus on open source, it's not too difficult to locate them. There are several methods to seek them out, listed here in order from least desirable to most desirable:

- Do a Web search listing the product you're interested in along with the phrase "professional services." Despite the ease of doing searches, it can be a bit of a challenge to find firms this way. Many of these firms focus more on technology than marketing, so they might not have used words that would make them come up in searches; that is, they might not be very savvy about search engine marketing techniques. This means they might not get listed at all, depending on the search terms you use. For example, they might use the term consulting rather than professional services; if you have used the latter, they might not appear at all in the resulting list, or could be buried several pages in. Try the search with a few other terms. With enough persistence and creativity, this method can produce some candidate professional services firms.

- If the product you're interested in has its own Web site, see if it has a listing of firms offering consulting services for the product. There is often a good relationship between the product developers and companies that offer consulting services, which can lead to a listing on the product's Web site. This is a form of implied endorsement from the product developers, which is good. Of course, this endorsement needs to be assessed, which is the subject of the next section. One of these firms might be a good candidate for services.

- Scan the product's e-mail archives to see if someone from a firm has posted frequently. Significant involvement with the product implies expertise, so the archives can be a good source of services firms.

- Post a query to the product e-mail list asking for recommendations. You're likely to get a biased response, which is to say that the responders are likely to be those who have had a positive experience. Again, assessment of the candidate firms is crucial.

If none of these methods turns up any candidates, you have several other options to identify services resources:

- Seek out individual consultants via the methods just listed. Using an individual consultant puts the burden on you, as you must retain responsibility for more aspects of the project. This approach will probably require you to rethink how you've organized the effort, but it could be a way to locate critical skills that you cannot supply.

- Contact the product development team and ask them if they have any sources for services. As noted earlier, there is often a good relationship between developers and knowledgeable product users. Even if there is nothing as formal as a Web site with services partners listed, the developers might be aware of an individual or a firm that can help.
- Contract directly with the development team for the services you need. This is not always an option, as the developers might have other commitments, but this can be an excellent way of obtaining services. It can also be very positive for developing a relationship with the developers, which can have significant benefits for the organization, as it builds a connection with the people who are responsible for the product and can ensure that the organization gets priority attention for its problems. However, with respect to professional services, you should be aware that the team's expertise is in product development, not project management. Consequently, you should treat this resource like using an individual consultant and think of it in the same way. This option will require you to take on more responsibility for project management and coordination.

One of these methods should identify professional services resources that you can use on your project. If none are available, you need to assess your overall project plan. If you have internal resources you can use to replace the services you were planning to obtain from an outside firm, you at least have an option. The question that then must be addressed is very familiar: What is the highest priority work for those individuals? Depending on the answer, you might choose to shift the resources and continue with the project.

If you can't find a professional services firm, there might still be other options.

If there are no internal resources available, and your search for outside services has been fruitless, I believe you are at an impasse. Perhaps this is a sign that you should seek out another product.

Assessing Professional Services Maturity

Assessing a professional services firm is critical before beginning work.

Finding a professional services partner gets you only halfway home. It's vitally important that the firm do quality work on your project. Without rehashing all the things that can go wrong when an incompetent firm works on a project, it's obvious that an incompetent firm is worse than no firm at all.

Assessing a local or regional firm poses some problems.

Assessing open-source–focused professional services firms can be tricky. They don't have brand-name awareness like the largest firms, so you might have to overcome some internal misgivings during the assessment phase. Just as you might be a bit uncomfortable purchasing a product from a manufacturer you're not familiar with, you might be hesitant to work with a services partner you've never heard of before. It's a natural reaction.

Assuming you can overcome your misgivings, there are some things to keep in mind:

- They're probably a small firm, so you need to be sure in your discussions with them that they have personnel available—truly available—to work on your project. You don't want your project delayed because the one person they have who is an expert on your product is busy somewhere else.
- They will probably be more technically adept than process-oriented. You should keep this in mind in all your dealings with them. Working with them will require more project management skills in your project team. Also, you'll need to insist on project-oriented requirements, which the firm might treat as unimportant. Documentation of the product's

configuration and any changes made to it are critical. As pointed out in the last chapter, this kind of documentation is often overlooked, which causes problems later.

- As a corollary to the last point, they might not be as polished as the firms you've worked with in the past. In fact, they might seem positively geekish. This might not be bad at all, if you're using them for specific skills.

On the other hand, there are some real benefits to working with a smaller firm. They might not have the style of large firms, but they tend to bring real substance to what they do. The positives of working with one of these firms are as follows:

Working with smaller firms can be very positive.

- They will be very responsive to your needs. You represent a significant part of their revenues, so you're an important customer. Your call will reach somebody who can make something happen. The large firms bring more polish, but it can be difficult to get attention paid to your project, unless it's really big.
- They are probably really technically adept with the product in question. They can very likely solve problems that your personnel or a larger firm's personnel would take significantly longer to address. There's nothing more comforting than knowing that a problem you refer is really going to be solved—right away.
- They will be very cost-efficient. They don't have the overhead of the larger firms—big marketing budgets, impressive offices, and seminars in exotic locations. This can translate into lower fees to you.

Because these firms are not as well known, a careful assessment is very important. Committing to a firm before you're completely comfortable with it can be a real mistake. Under no circumstances

It's vital to do a thorough assessment.

should you select an open source professional services firm before you have thoroughly vetted its credentials.

Review your project plan with the firm.

The first step is to outline your project plans. If they do not respond positively to your project approach and offer a complementary working style to yours, beware. As already noted, some firms are much more technical and less process oriented; they might just want to roll up their sleeves and get to work. It never gets any better than the first meeting in terms of a firm offering to work your way. If it seems like your working styles are not in sync, don't compromise. Walking away now is less painful than walking away after lots of work and money.

Be sure to check references.

Assuming it seems like the two organizations' working styles mesh, check references. These firms should have rave reviews from their customers, because their size and passion should make their working relationships very productive. When checking references, probe on questions of working style, thoroughness of ancillary project items like documentation, and schedule timeliness. If the project is going to be turned over to your organization at the end, check to see how well project hand-offs have been handled.

Ask for an opinion about the product in question.

Confirm that the firm has expertise in your product. Knowing a lot about one open source product doesn't translate into expertise on all open source products. Ask for their impression of the pros and cons of the product you've selected. The depth of the answers is very informative about the firm's quality of thinking and lets you know how much knowledge of the product is spread throughout the organization.

Review a sample project plan from one of the firm's other projects.

Review a sample project plan from another project. The detail and organization will say a lot about how well the company plans its work. Organizations, just like people, don't usually change, so if you're not impressed with the quality of work done for others, you probably won't be impressed with whatever is done for you.

Ask to see a proposed project plan for your project. If you do choose to work with the firm, strongly consider breaking the projects into phases. Have the first phase be relatively short (a project assessment and design phase is usually a good-sized chunk of work) with a deliverable that can be assessed for quality and timeliness.

As to see a proposed plan for your project.

Based on all of this, you should have a good sense of the quality of the firm and whether it will be a good partner on your project. Being small and unknown isn't necessarily a warning sign for you to avoid a professional services firm; neither is it an endorsement of its quality. Satisfy yourself as to its abilities and references before you sign the engagement letter.

Satisfy yourself about the firm before signing a contract.

Assigning a Professional Services Maturity Score

One question you might have is whether the maturity of a product's professional services should be assessed if you are not planning to make use of them. I recommend that you do because the availability and maturity of professional services for a product imply a great deal about the product's maturity, whether or not you actually use services at all.

Assign a services maturity score even if you plan to do all the work yourself.

It's easy to understand why with a bit of reflection. The purpose of the OSMM is to assess the maturity level of a product, which correlates very strongly with the size of the user community. For the reasons discussed in the overview earlier in this chapter, professional services firms only begin working with a product when they believe the product has a large user base that is willing to invest in services. Therefore, assessing the maturity of a product's professional services options is a valuable way to help assess the product's overall

The availability of professional services is strongly correlated with product maturity.

maturity. This is why it makes sense to assess this element, even if you do not plan to take advantage of any services. Of course, project plans often change midstream, sometimes requiring incorporating outside resources, so there is a pragmatic reason to evaluate the services available for a product during the maturity assessment phase as well.

There are 10 potential points for professional services maturity.

Table 10.1 outlines the potential point assignment for professional services. If there are services available from the product team or a product-based commercial entity, three points are possible. For example, our example product JBoss has services offered by its parent company (see Table 10.2 for JBoss's services evaluation). If local or regional firms offer services for the product as well, an additional four points are possible. Finally, if a large national or global firm offers services, an additional three points can be added. As noted earlier, to this point the largest professional service firms have not committed to open source products other than Linux, but they undoubtedly will over the next year or so. If one of these firms does offer services for the product under evaluation, it is a very strong maturity indicator.

Table 10.1
Professional Services Maturity Score

Element	Score
Product team offers services	3
Services available from local or regional firms	4
Services available from national or international firms	3
Professional services possible maturity score	10

Assessing JBoss: Professional Services

The assessment process for JBoss regarding professional services is outlined in Table 10.3 on page 220. The JBoss OSMM score for the chapter is listed in Table 10.2.

JBoss itself offers services, including strategy and architecture. In addition, JBoss has a number of professional services partners that specialize in the product. In examining the Web sites of several of the providers, the following factors are generally true:

JBoss itself offers professional services along with a number of other service providers.

- The firms are quite small and are focused on deep Java technology skills.
- They are located around the world, but tend to be local firms, with one to three locations (one being most prevalent).
- No good-sized professional services firm appears to proclaim significant JBoss expertise.

From this, it can be concluded that professional services are available for the product; however, the client will need to retain significant responsibility for project management and architectural direction. Because the firms lack project management capabilities, only three of the four possible points have been assigned.

You will need to retain significant responsibility for management and direction.

Element	Score
Product team offers services	3
Services available from local or regional firms	3
Services available from national or international firms	0
Professional services maturity score	6

Table 10.2
JBoss Professional Services Maturity Score

Table 10.3   OSMM Professional Services Assessment Checklist

<table>
<tr><td colspan="2" align="center">OPEN SOURCE MATURITY MODEL
Professional Services Assessment Checklist</td></tr>
<tr><td colspan="2">Product Name: JBoss</td></tr>
<tr><td align="center">Method</td><td align="center">Notes</td></tr>
<tr><td colspan="2" align="center">Professional Services</td></tr>
<tr>
<td>Examined JBoss.com site for information regarding professional services.</td>
<td>JBoss has JASP (JBoss Authorized Service Partner Program), which endorses professional service providers for product.

Program lists 11 JASP partners located throughout the world, all small to medium-sized firms.</td>
</tr>
<tr>
<td>Performed Google search on "JBoss consulting" and located approximately 20 more firms claiming JBoss consulting expertise.</td>
<td>Firms are located throughout the world. All are small to medium-sized firms.

Professional services appear to be available in nearly any location, but might require travel on the part of consultants.</td>
</tr>
<tr>
<td>Examined Web sites of several of the professional services firms identified in the previous two methods.</td>
<td>All of the firms are quite small and are implementation focused, meaning their strength lies in technology, rather than strategy or process.

The amount of direct experience with JBoss appears to range from slight to extensive.</td>
</tr>
</table>

11

JBoss Open Source Maturity
Model Assessment

Executive Summary

The purpose of the OSMM is to assist organizations as they select, evaluate, and implement open source software. The OSMM identifies the key elements that IT organizations need to succeed with open source and provides a four-step process to evaluate each element for its maturity level. After each element has been evaluated, weightings are applied to each element to calculate an overall maturity score for the product.

This chapter brings our example OSMM evaluation to a conclusion. Each chapter in this section of the book has described one element of a mature open source product. Each chapter has also presented a sample evaluation of that element for our example product, JBoss. Now we can move on to combining the evaluations for each element into an overall assessment of JBoss's maturity.

Another purpose of the OSMM is to highlight aspects of the product that need improvement or areas an organization needs to address to prepare for using an open source product. By comparing how a product measures up in the different elements, it might become clear that one element lags the maturity of the others and requires some mitigation. In this way, the OSMM acts as more than a scorecard, but also acts as a signpost offering direction.

A completed OSMM for JBoss is presented here, along with an analysis of its implications. Some aspects of the product that need attention are identified, together with some methods that an organization might use to address them.

Review of the JBoss OSMM Assessment

The JBoss evaluation in this book provides an example of an OSMM assessment.

The purpose of evaluating JBoss in this book is to provide a real-world example of the maturity assessment process. To that end, each element of a mature product has been assessed, with the appropriate checklist filled out, listing evaluation methods along with significant information identified in a notes section.

The element checklists highlight strengths and weaknesses of a product.

The appropriate use of the checklists during the final evaluation phase is to examine any areas that show shortcomings in the product or highlight areas the organization itself needs to address. Each element and any relevant notes are discussed next.

The score for each element as well as an overall maturity score for JBoss is contained in Table 11.1.

Table 11.1
JBoss OSMM Score

Element	Potential Score	Actual Score	Weighting Factor	Element Weighted Score
Software	10	8	4	32
Technical support	10	8	2	16
Documentation	10	6	1	6
Training	10	8	1	8
Integration	10	10	1	10
Professional services	10	6	1	6
Total product maturity score				78

JBoss Software

JBoss product functionality is easy to assess and quite complete.

It is relatively easy to assess JBoss functionality, as it adheres to the J2EE standard. In fact, it will certify against the Sun J2EE 1.4 Compatibility Test Suite in 2004, which is the official method of determining J2EE standards compliance. Therefore, its functionality is quite complete with respect to J2EE compliance. It suffers in comparison with the main commercial providers of J2EE application servers, as they have created products to extend the standard to differentiate themselves from their competitors. In particular, the commercial vendors offer specialized IDEs for their products that raise programmer productivity and thereby lower the total cost of ownership (TCO) for their products. On the other hand, these IDEs create vendor lock-in, which is one of the things that using a standards-based product is supposed to prevent. Overall, JBoss matches up well to commercial providers of J2EE application servers.

JBoss's product longevity is somewhat shorter than commercial alternatives. They have been around one to two years longer than JBoss. As noted in the Chapter 5, "The Open Source Product," however, JBoss has had a very large number of downloads (4.4 million), which tends to mitigate the longevity advantage of its competitors.

> JBoss has good product longevity; its commercial counterparts have somewhat greater longevity.

In terms of product quality, JBoss stacks up quite well. It has a large number of tests. Inspection of the tests themselves indicates good test quality. The JBoss team will perform the J2EE certification test suite in 2004, which adds a significant number (more than 16,000) of tests to the overall test suite. Unfortunately, it was not feasible to perform a test coverage assessment during this product evaluation, so determining what proportion of the product has been touched by QA tests has not been done.

> JBoss product quality is quite good.

The JBoss product team is very large for an open source product. It has very talented engineers with significant commercial experience. Out of a list of 91 team members, the number of active engineers (consistently checking in code) is about a dozen, which is still a good-sized team for an open source product.

> The JBoss development team is large.

Overall, JBoss stacks up quite well as a product, which is reflected in its 8 points out of a potential total of 10.

JBoss Technical Support

JBoss has a
number of
community
mailing lists.

JBoss has a very large and active user community. JBoss.org offers a number of support forums that are quite active. In addition, the commercial arm of the JBoss project, JBoss.com offers commercial support for JBoss (indeed, support is the main source of its revenues).

A drawback is
that some mailing
list postings do
not receive
responses.

The main caveat with respect to the user community and its support is the fact that many postings do not receive responses from anyone. This could imply lethargy on the part of the community, but an organization considering JBoss would need to look into this issue. A low percentage of JBoss users purchase commercial support, which implies most users rely on the support forums. If your organization were considering going that route, it would be important to understand why so many postings go unanswered.

JBoss offers two
types of
commercial
support, delivered
via e-mail and
phone. It appears
that on-site
support might
now be available.

JBoss.com provides two different types of commercial support: development and production. The former is available to help with usage problems that come up during application creation, whereas the latter is oriented toward production groups that are responsible for keeping J2EE applications up and running. JBoss employs the most active JBoss developers in the community and uses them to deliver both types of support. From the perspective of a user, it doesn't get much better than having the person who wrote the code available for consultation. This is a great benefit for JBoss users and should be strongly considered, especially by those organizations that plan to use the product in mission-critical applications. The sole drawback to this support is that it is available by phone only; JBoss at this time does not offer on-site service. That might change in the future; it would be worthwhile discussing that during contract negotiations. (JBoss recently announced that it now offers on-site support. It was too late to perform an assessment of its quality, but if it is as good as the development and product support already offered, it should be more than acceptable.) Because of the very active user community and the fact that JBoss itself offers technical support, this element is assigned a score of eight.

JBoss Documentation

As noted in Chapter 7, "Open Source Documentation," JBoss is unusual because the project team funded creation of high-quality documentation by selling it, rather than giving it away as is common for most other open source projects. Even though the documentation is quite inexpensive, the total revenues sufficed to support the technical writer who created it. Many postings, both in product forums and Web sites, praised the for-pay documentation. On the other hand, many people criticized the free documentation available with the product; among the complaints were poor writing, incompleteness, and obsolescence. This reinforces the observation made in Chapter 7 that open source software engineers do not create very good documentation.

> JBoss is unusual in that the product documentation is thorough and well written.

In addition, there are many Web postings that provide product documentation. The quality of these postings ranges from poor to excellent; many of the postings are poorly written or sketchy in terms of thoroughness.

> The quality of JBoss Web-based postings varies.

The main shortfall of JBoss documentation has nothing to do with the product or the company itself. The documentation sold by commercial publishers is criticized very strongly on Amazon.com for reasons of originality and accuracy. One or two others are due out by the end of 2004, so this situation will probably improve significantly.

> JBoss commercial documentation is problematic; however, it should improve shortly.

If your organization were considering using JBoss, it would be important to invest in the for-pay project documentation, at the least. Documentation for other J2EE products could be used, but the configuration and administration of each J2EE product varies widely, so much of the documentation for other products would

> The product documentation should be purchased as the product is very complex.

not apply to JBoss. The free documentation available with the product should not be used for the reasons just outlined. Whatever documentation the organization settles on, it should be made available to everyone. J2EE application servers are very complex; trying to create and run a J2EE application without documentation is foolhardy.

The overall documentation score for JBoss is reduced due to the mixed quality of the Web-based postings and commercial documentation.

Although the product documentation prepared by the team is quite good, the maturity score of this element was reduced due to the fact that the community postings on the Web are relatively low. Also, despite the fact that commercial documentation is available (ordinarily a very strong sign of product maturity), its quality is poor, which reduces the points assigned for this item. Overall, JBoss documentation receives 6 points out of a total of 10.

JBoss Training

JBoss has many training options available.

There are many training options for JBoss, available online, in printed format, and in the classroom. JBoss.com itself delivers high-quality training as one of its services. There is yet another option: training on a commercial product that is applicable to an open source product. This option is certainly available for JBoss, as a number of commercial training entities, both private and public (in the sense of educational institutions) provide training on commercial J2EE products.

JBoss receives a training score of 8 out of 10 possible points.

JBoss received a very high score for this product element, as training is widely available. The only area that did not receive a full set of points was commercial tutorials. This is because there is a relative paucity of commercial documentation as of the writing of this book. Several books are due out over the next year, which should address this shortcoming. The maturity score of JBoss's training is 8.

The widespread availability of training is a very positive sign for JBoss. J2EE application servers are very complex; it is a true challenge to learn how to effectively program and administer Enterprise JavaBeans. Any organization contemplating moving to J2EE should carefully assess its employee skill sets to see what training gaps need to be addressed. Hoping that employees will pick up J2EE skills informally by reading on their own time would be a dangerous approach. Any IT organization that might use JBoss should take advantage of the training available for it.

Training for a product as complex as JBoss is critical.

JBoss Integration with Other Products

Product integrations are very site specific; a real software infrastructure must be used to determine what integrations a product requires. Because this OSMM assessment is an example, an idealized software stack was used as the basis for assessing JBoss. There are a wide variety of integration mechanisms available for JBoss. Furthermore, many integrations with commercial software products have been created by vendors; this was discussed in Chapter 9, "Open Source Integration with Other Products," as a strong implication of product maturity. Because of these two factors, JBoss was assigned a perfect 10 out of 10 in this category.

JBoss has outstanding integration capabilities.

JBoss Professional Services

Organizations considering JBoss have a number of different professional services options. The parent company offers services, as do a fairly large number of consulting firms spread throughout the world. If your organization cannot find a satisfactory firm, there are many experienced JBoss engineers available to work on a consulting basis. As of today, no large firms offer JBoss-based services, but that might change in the near future as the product becomes better established.

JBoss offers professional services, as do a number of small local and regional firms.

Be aware that you will need to retain overall project management responsibilities.

If you plan to take advantage of professional services for any JBoss efforts your organization undertakes, you should carefully consider your requirements. The professional services available are engineering-oriented, rather than strategic or even project-management–oriented. Depending on your requirements, these firms might serve you very well; however, you would need to be clear about what you need and explicitly assess whether the firm in question can deliver. Reference checking would need to be performed thoroughly.

JBoss received a services score of 6 out of 10 possible points.

Because the firms that provide services are small and engineering-centric, and also because no large firms current offer consulting services, this element is assigned a score of 6 out of 10.

Assessing the JBoss OSMM Score

The overall OSMM score for JBoss is 78 out of 100 possible points.

JBoss's total score on the OSMM is 78 points (please refer to Table 11.1). Comparing this score with the recommended minimum OSMM scores (Table 11.2), you can see that the JBoss maturity score qualifies it to be used in production environments by both early adopter and pragmatist IT organizations. Both types of organizations could move forward to a pilot stage with JBoss, confident that it "penciled out" at a sufficient maturity level.

Table 11.2
Recommended Minimum OSMM Scores

Purpose of Use	Type of User	
	Early Adopter	Pragmatist
Experimentation	25	40
Pilot	40	60
Production	60	70

Even after an OSMM evaluation of JBoss, a pilot test is appropriate.

It would still be important to perform a pilot test with JBoss, as organization- or environment-specific factors might show up during testing. However, because of the OSMM score, it is unlikely that the product would be found totally unacceptable during a pilot. Failing to perform a pilot test would be imprudent on the part of the organization.

Comments on the OSMM Process

The OSMM is designed to shorten the time needed to determine whether a particular product should undergo more detailed assessment. Because of the loose coupling of the product elements that make up a mature product, open source products are more difficult to assess for maturity. The OSMM is designed to reduce the burden of this process and make it possible for a small team to assess the product in a short period of time. A second reason for the OSMM is to make the process more explicit; that is, to document the findings of the process in a way that allows the organization to identify product weaknesses and to plan for mitigating actions.

The OSMM shortens the product assessment process.

The JBoss assessment that serves as an example in this book took one individual about two weeks to perform. This chapter reviewed each product element and identified several areas that, although not significant enough to lower JBoss's maturity score to an unacceptable level, did need attention. For a small investment of time and money, the OSMM offers significant benefits in helping organizations evaluate open source products.

The JBoss assessment in this book required only two person-weeks to perform.

If this JBoss OSMM assessment were real, the sponsoring organization would find it quite easy to identify a number of action items to be pursued with the JBoss organization as well as other service providers. It would be much easier to create a project plan based, in part, on the findings of this OSMM.

The JBoss OSMM assessment has identified a number of items that need to be addressed.

Conclusion

Writing a book is a temporal activity. Even in the best of circumstances, a year passes between preparing a book proposal and physical books being available at local bookstores. I began this project based on my firm's experience working with clients, convinced that companies would increasingly move to open source solutions. When people asked me why I was writing a book about how IT organizations could methodically select, assess, and implement open source software, I would reply, jokingly, "Open source is ready for the airplane ride experience." When they looked at me quizzically, I would elaborate: "The CEO of the company walks into the CIO's office and says 'I was on an airplane last week and read an article about open source—what are we doing about it?' and the CIO realizes the organization needs to get going on open source. Well, this book will offer a formalized process to successfully bring open source solutions into IT organizations."

Midway through writing this book, that scenario became real when *Fortune* magazine published an extensive article on open source, discussing its importance and detailing why companies were moving toward open source solutions ("How the Open-Source World Plans to Smack Down Microsoft, and Oracle, and . . . ," *Fortune*, February 23, 2004, p. 92). I can only imagine the many discussions that ensued as a result of that article. It's startling to see one's offhand remarks take on a life of their own.

Nothing has happened during the past year to convince me that the use of open source will stop growing exponentially. Its control, flexibility, quality, and cost-effectiveness will drive organizations to open source solutions. The need to make IT investment available for vital business solutions and innovative new technologies will give open source a perennial place on the annual "Top 10 IT Trends" articles published each January.

Everything that has happened with open source during the past year reinforces my conviction that IT organizations will find the formalized process of the OSMM useful as they implement open source software. As companies put open source products through the OSMM assessment process, I encourage them to share their product ratings with other members of the community at the OSMM section of my firm's Web site, *www.navicasoft.com*. Every assessment my firm completes will (with our client's permission) be posted there. One of the greatest strengths of open source is the shared knowledge of the community; I hope that making OSMM assessments easily available will contribute to the community.

As mentioned in the Preface, I would be delighted to hear from readers about their experiences (both good and bad) with the OSMM and this book. I can be reached by e-mail at *bgolden@ navicasoft.com*.

Bibliography

DiBona, Chris, et al. *Open Sources: Voices from the Open Source Revolution.* Sebastapol, CA: O'Reilly & Associates, 1999.

> A collection of essays from many of the notables of the open source movement. A single source to see the range of opinions present in the open source community.

Fink, Martin. *The Business and Economics of Linux and Open Source.* Upper Saddle River, NJ: Prentice Hall, 2003.

> An overview of open source from the perspective of a commercial technology provider. Analyzes open source economics when intellectual property is shared rather than hoarded.

Pavlicek, Russell. *Embracing Insanity: Open Source Software Development.* Indianapolis, IN: Sams Publishing, 2000.

> Open source software from the perspective of the developer.

Raymond, Eric. *The Cathedral & the Bazaar.* Sebastapol, CA: O'Reilly & Associates, 2001.

> Essays on what motivates open source developers, why open source does not mean noncommercial, and more. A bracing introduction to the open source culture.

Rosen, Lawrence. *Open Source Licensing: Software Freedom and Intellectual Property Law.* Indianapolis, IN: Prentice Hall PTR, 2005.

> A thorough and easily comprehensible overview of open source software licenses and their implications. Also contains a description of many of the most common software licenses.

Weber, Steven. *The Success of Open Source.* Cambridge, MA: Harvard University Press, 2004.

> A political scientist looks at the open source phenomenon and explains why open source communities work, despite the lack of monetary exchange.

Index